Public Scholarship in Literary Studies

Edited by

RACHEL ARTEAGA
ROSEMARY ERICKSON JOHNSEN

Amherst College Press
Amherst, Massachusetts

Copyright © 2021 by Rachel Arteaga and Rosemary Erickson Johnsen

This work is licensed under the Creative Commons Attribution- NoDerivatives 4.0 International License. To view a copy of this license, visit http://creativecommons.org/licenses/by-nd/4.0/ or send a letter to Creative Commons, PO Box 1866, Mountain View, CA 94042, USA.

DOI: https://doi.org/10.3998/mpub.12225223
ISBN 978-1-943208-22-7 (paper)
ISBN978- 1-943207-23-4 (OA)

Cover photography courtesy of Rosemary Erickson Johnsen, 2017.

Published in the United States of America by
Amherst College Press
Manufactured in the United States of America

CONTENTS

List of Illustrations	v
Acknowledgments	vii
Introduction Rachel Arteaga	1
Public Scholarship in the Age of the Christian Right: A Self-Interested Tale Christopher Douglas	17
What Lasts Cynthia L. Haven	43
Takin' It to the Streets: Public Scholarship in the Heartland Carmaletta M. Williams	57
Linking Classrooms, Connecting Learning: The University of Washington Texts and Teachers Program Gary Handwerk, Anu Taranath, and Christine Chaney	71
Lifting the Color Curtain with the Clemente Course in the Humanities Jim Cocola	91
Dancing with the Inductive: The Emergence of a Centre for Community Engaged Narrative Arts Daniel Coleman and Lorraine York	111
Conclusion: Literary Study Writ Large Rosemary Erickson Johnsen	145
Appendix: Program Overviews	153
List of Contributors	155

LIST OF ILLUSTRATIONS

Public Scholarship in the Age of the Christian Right: A Self-Interested Tale

Figure 1. *The Conversation's* pitch page. *Source*: *The Conversation*, https://theconversation.com/us.   21

Figure 2. My fifteen minutes. *Source*: Christopher Douglas, "The Religious Origins of Fake News and "Alternative Facts," *Religion Dispatches*, 23 Feb. 2017.   24

Figure 3. Not your parents' dystopian *Friends*. *Source*: Christopher Douglas, "Why America's Handmaid's Tale Doesn't Look like Hulu's," *Religion Dispatches*, 2018.   30

Figure 4. Social media as public scholarship. *Source*: *Twitter*.   32

Figure 5. Occasion, copyright, reprinting. *Source*: Christopher Douglas, "The Unfilmable 'Blood Meridian,'" *The Conversation*, 11 Mar. 2018.   34

Lifting the Color Curtain with the Clemente Course in the Humanities

Figure 1. Poetry session on *The Epic of Gilgamesh*, 25 Feb. 2016.   93

Figure 2. The Bard College Clemente Course in the Humanities, Worcester, Massachusetts.   93

Figure 3. J. M. W. Turner, *Slavers Throwing Overboard the Dead and Dying, Typhoon Coming On*, 1840. Oil on Canvas, 35.7 in. × 48.3 in. *Source*: Museum of Fine Arts, Boston.   105

Dancing with the Inductive: The Emergence of a Centre for Community Engaged Narrative Arts

Figure 1. The long table. *Source*: Lorraine York. 123
Figure 2. The long table. *Source*: Lorraine York. 124
Figure 3. One of the works reproduced in Rick Hill's book. Shelley Niro, Kanien'kehaka (Mohawk), *Skywoman*, 2001. Foam, fiberglass resin, oil paint, canvas, and metal. *Source*: Canadian Museum of Civilization, 2000.129.1.1-10, D2004-11229. 133
Figure 4. Klyde Broox. *Source*: Lorraine York. 135
Figure 5. "Tree Versus Battery Cases" by Cees van Gemerden. *Source*: Cees van Gemerden. 138
Figure 6. The general public chance upon the *No Trespassing* installation at Hamilton's Aquafest, 1990. *Source*: Annerie van Gemerden. 137
Figure 7. Margaret Flood, *Something Round*. *Source*: Wendy Coleman. 143

ACKNOWLEDGMENTS

Rachel Arteaga and Rosemary Erickson Johnsen

Our first thanks go to our contributors, for without their willingness to share their expertise and experience, this volume would not exist. We hope readers find their essays as compelling and inspirational as we do. Their generosity in sharing their work was matched by their flexibility and responsiveness to editorial suggestions; all were a pleasure to work with. Beth Bouloukos at Amherst College Press provided answers, encouragement, and never-flagging energy for our project; she was the champion it needed throughout the process of moving from a great idea to a completed volume. The anonymous readers for the press offered practical suggestions and encouragement, and their work made the finished volume better.

* * *

Rachel: This volume of essays began as a response to two questions posed by Kathleen Woodward in a 2009 *Dædalus* article on the future of the humanities: What would public literary scholarship mean? What would a public literary criticism look like? These questions have informed and inspired my work on this project and in my role at the Simpson Center for the Humanities, a space on the University of Washington campus that is defined by rigorous scholarly practices, a commitment to the inherent and public value of humanities research and teaching, and a spirit of generosity. For her incisive questions and critiques, for her insistence on the importance of disciplinary specificity—which honors both the content and the methods at stake in any tradition of scholarly work—and for her leadership in building the intellectual and institutional infrastructures through which so much extraordinary public scholarship has been made possible on and beyond our campus, I give Kathy my grateful thanks.

In collaboration with the Simpson Center and many other partners, Miriam Bartha and Bruce Burgett have decisively built up and together sustained the graduate certificate in public scholarship at the University of Washington; their key arguments about the meanings and practices of publicly engaged research convinced me early on in my doctoral studies in English that public scholarship in literary studies was possible, necessary, and serious work. For her mentorship and her immensely creative and generous thinking, I am deeply indebted to Miriam. I would like to also thank the Simpson Center staff, especially Annie Dwyer, whose work in public scholarship and doctoral education reform inspires me every day. Public scholarship is based in strong relationships, and I am grateful for individuals across the many communities of practice in which my own work has been shaped, especially the faculty and doctoral students who have participated as fellows in the Mellon-funded Reimagining the Humanities PhD and Reaching New Publics: Catalyzing Collaboration program, our partners in the Seattle district community colleges, and my colleagues locally and nationally who work directly in and for the public humanities, from Humanities Washington to the National Humanities Alliance.

My identification with the professional study of literature began in a high school English classroom. To those teachers—first among them, in my life, Dr. Jeffrey Dunn—whose commitment to literary studies as a truly public good is demonstrated through careers in public education, I give my deepest thanks. Finally, a word of thanks to Brandon Arteaga for his support and his unyielding belief in the importance of this work in the world.

* * *

Rosemary: Public scholarship cannot happen without invitations, opportunities, and support, and for all of these I would like to thank Suzanne Ross and Maura Junius of the Raven Foundation; Ben Railton of Fitchburg State University, the past president of NeMLA; and Andrew Nestingen, the chair of the University of Washington's Department of Scandinavian Studies. Over the course of this project's development, presentations about public scholarship at two MLA conventions, the National Humanities Conference, the Society for the Advancement of Scandinavian Study, the American Association of State Colleges and Universities, and the Council for Adult and Experiential Learning's Chicagoland Veterans Higher Education Affinity Group provided opportunities to share with, and learn from, others in the field. Two National Endowment for the Humanities grant projects made a terrific platform for public-humanities engagement and created opportunities for Governors State University students and student-veterans to become public scholars in their own right. Heartfelt thanks to all of them, especially the team who took their public scholarship to the community: Akya Gossit, Brandon Green, Eden Puente, Kristi Schaefer, Aidah Abdullah, Ami Henderson, and Haley Walsh. Thanks also to my NEH project collaborators at GSU, Dean Andrae Marak and Director of Veterans Affairs Kevin Smith. As my concluding essay in this volume indicates, the MLA's Committee on the Status of Women in the Profession (CSWP) provided concepts, motivation, and opportunities for me to engage with public scholarship, not just as something I do but as something to examine and promote systematically. Thanks to all of the CSWP members with whom I served, but especially my two "sister cochairs," Jean E. Howard and Carmaletta Williams, and Lisa Surwillo. I have been fortunate to have as long-time mentors who affirmed the value of my scholarship in all of its forms Martha J. Reineke of the University of Northern Iowa and the late Douglas Noverr of Michigan State University. My family has been partner to my public scholarship and contributor to keeping the show on the road joyfully: words cannot express what I owe to my husband Bill and to our children, Lenna and Arnold, who have grown up alongside the practice of public scholarship in literary studies.

Introduction

Rachel Arteaga

We have collected in this volume a set of compelling and successful approaches to public scholarship in literary studies, which can be read both as notes toward the future of the discipline and as case studies of the publicly engaged humanities more broadly. All of the publications, teaching engagements, partnerships, and projects represented in this collection are models for others to learn from and, in their own ways, to follow. As coeditors of this volume, Rosemary Erickson Johnsen and I have made no attempt to comprehensively describe the landscape of public scholarship as it exists in English departments across the United States and Canada today.[1] And it has not been our ambition to map out the innumerable contributions to public life that have been made by professionals who have been, at any level of their education, trained in English departments as majors, masters, or doctorates.[2] Instead, we have focused on these six exemplary works we received from the field as indicators of an increasing interest among scholars in literary studies, however positioned, to turn toward, engage with, and learn from various publics beyond the academy.

A decade ago, literary critic Kathleen Woodward posed the essential questions on which the entire discussion turns: "What would public literary scholarship mean? What would a public literary criticism look like?" ("Future" 120). In publishing this collection of works, we revisit these questions and expand upon them, to discover and to demonstrate the ways in which the public practice of literary criticism proliferates today and to invite our readers to offer—and to creatively imagine—their own answers. One of our findings is that the full range of expertise within literary studies must be included in the discussion. The public stakes of the academic study of literary texts are simply too high to limit ourselves to the practice, however defined, of literary criticism. Based on the range of work being done by our contributing writers—within and across institutions where literature is taught and studied; in public community spaces and for audiences not traditionally recognized as full participants in the production of new knowledge in the humanities; across forms, genres, and new media platforms—we feel that it is important for readers to consider literary criticism as only one part of a larger whole.

In his landmark institutional history *Professing Literature* (1987), Gerald Graff describes the internal conflicts that shaped English departments in colleges and universities as they were being established in the United States. As many of our readers will intimately know, these debates took many forms and their implications persist to the present day. Among the central preoccupations observable in the debates, as Graff tracks them through institutional communications and public remarks, is a question: What dignifies the profession? Is it, as many professors in the late nineteenth and early twentieth century agreed, specialization and a rigorous methodology, a form of scientific inquiry? Or, as others argued in response, is the profession dignified by its traditions of teaching and learning and its relationship to students, classrooms, and canons? In either case, the elevation of reading literature from a leisure activity, as it was commonly understood, to a professionalized activity performed by individuals with specialized training was a formative ideal for English departments in their inception (68). And, as Deidre Lynch argues in her more recent (and more far-reaching) history of English studies, *Loving Literature: A Cultural History* (2015), "[T]hose of us for whom English is a line of work are also called upon to love literature and to ensure that others do so too" (1). She writes,

> The many accounts we have of the professionalization of literary study and criticism are incomplete without a consideration of literature's *personalization* and the practices and institutions of reading by which it was supported. For a start, that narrative leaves us unable to assess the entanglements of the institutional and the intimate within the informal, everyday practice of English studies, within that psycho-pedagogy of everyday life that defines the discipline's real effectivity just as much as our publications in literary criticism do. (12)

Many scholars of literary studies are doing their work today, in part, in this terrain of everyday life. Their projects in public scholarship engage new readerships, students, and community partners in often very personal terms, with high stakes, involving identity, belonging, and deeply held beliefs. In short, by seeking out the entanglements of the professional and the personal, the institutional and the intimate, that public scholarship makes possible, scholars in literary studies have much to gain in terms of a renewed understanding of the meaning and purpose of this work in the world. As is evident in the chapters to follow, they also have much to contribute. Alongside the writers of the six chapters in this volume, in honor of the work of all publicly engaged scholars of literary studies, and in the context of this historical moment, we propose an answer to the question of what dignifies our profession today. It is dignified by its long-standing commitments to intellectual depth, interpretive range, and rigorous attention to texts and contexts—and, equally, by its many meaningful and generous contributions to the public good.

* * *

As is so often the case in the most important debates in our profession, conversations about public scholarship in literary studies have been animated by the process of defining key terms. This process has produced important questions. Among them: What is public scholarship? How can we define the public humanities? Are these distinct and, if so, how can they be usefully identified as such? Are these engagements, however labelled, authentically scholarly? If so, by what standards and metrics will they be assessed, by whom, and for what purposes? These questions and all that they imply are still very much being answered, in practice as much as in theory. In an introduction to a recent collection of essays in *Post45* on the theme of "public humanities as/and comparatist practice," Ricardo Ortiz, chair and associate professor of Latinx literature in the English department of Georgetown University, suggests that public humanities may be "a discipline, an intellectual movement, a social justice movement, or a professional and institutional corrective to an unsustainable economic model in higher education," or, perhaps, "more than one or even all of these things at the same time." He acknowledges that "what public humanities is and how it best works in the world remains an open question" (Ortiz "Introduction"). The essays in that collection, and in ours, narrate publicly engaged humanistic inquiry through what I would describe as first-person practitioner accounts. What these chapters offer us is a concrete demonstration of the many approaches that can be taken to this work, what motivates it, and the results it produces in the discipline and in the world.

Yet, the terms in circulation are still very much worth considering. Public scholarship can be best understood as an ambitious and capacious approach to academic research, writing, and teaching. It indicates an expansive view of the impact that scholarly work in the humanities can have on society. Timothy Eatman, an educational sociologist and publicly engaged scholar who has been enormously influential in discussions of public scholarship in the United States in his role in developing the organization Imagining America: Artists and Scholars in Public Life (IA), and Julie Ellison, professor of English language and literature at the University of Michigan (and a founder, with historian David Scobey, of the organization), define public scholarship as "scholarly or creative activity integral to a faculty member's academic area" that also "encompasses different forms of making knowledge 'about, for, and with' diverse publics and communities." They continue, noting that "through a coherent, purposeful sequence of activities, it contributes to the public good and yields artifacts of public and intellectual value" ("Scholarship in Public" 1). In this definition, public scholarship must be informed by academic expertise while also being authentically accountable to diverse stakeholders beyond the scholarly audiences that traditionally facilitate and authorize the production of humanistic knowledge. For the work to be public, it must contribute to the public good; for the work to be scholarship, it must have intellectual value. Eatman and Ellison suggest that when these criteria are met, the activities of public scholarship can make significant contributions to scholarly discourse and to public life at the same time. This also means that the activities of public scholarship are accountable, both to scholarly communities, which have the power to assess the value of the work to a field of study, and to nonscholarly communities, which have the power to determine the relevance of the insights of the work for public and community life.

The public humanities might be understood more broadly, in that the activities described by the term do not necessarily reference the production of new academic research or involve faculty directly, even if those activities are fundamentally informed or inspired by humanities scholarship. In the United States, this kind of work is typified by the projects and programming of the state humanities councils, which were founded by the federal government as decentralized organizations able to make meaningful connections between humanities questions and concepts and communities in every state and territory of the nation. The National Foundation on the Arts and the Humanities Act of 1965 established the National Endowment for the Humanities (NEH) and the National Endowment for the Arts (NEA); the system of state councils was correspondingly established so that humanities programming would be made broadly accessible. The text of the act makes its motivating rationale clear, stating unequivocally that "the arts and the humanities belong to all the people of the United States ("National")." In Canada, the Social Sciences and Humanities Research Council (SSHRC), the federal research funding agency responsible for supporting research in the areas to which its title refers, uses similar language in describing its core values, stating that the agency is "committed to engaging its stakeholder communities and demonstrating that the research it supports leads to benefits for Canadians" ("Community"). Projects funded at this level are required to contribute to the public; all Canadians are meant to be the beneficiaries of the work that the SSHRC makes possible.

In her concise institutional history of the humanities, "Serious Work," Miriam Bartha, director of graduate programs and strategic initiatives for the School of Interdisciplinary Arts & Sciences at the University of Washington Bothell, writes, "[T]he rubric of the 'public humanities' that emerged in the late 1980s and 1990s responded to the 'crisis in the humanities' of the same period and sought to reorient the work of academic scholarship in concert with other professional sectors identified with the humanities such as museums, libraries, and state humanities councils" (Bartha 88). During these years, and with a similar ethos, humanities centers and institutes were rapidly established in institutions of higher education around the world, especially in the United States and Canada; many of them developed programming with explicitly public aims (88). In this account, new institutional formations emerged to bring humanities scholarship into alignment with the founding vision of the NEH and the organizations and institutions that, from their beginnings, had been oriented toward public audiences. In this sense, we might give priority to the term *public humanities*, both for the precedents it sets for public value and ownership of humanistic knowledge and for its expansive sense of audience, while turning to the term *public scholarship* to specify projects more narrowly when we can say with conviction that they both contribute to an area of scholarship and to the public good.

* * *

While attending a session on trends in humanities research at the convention of the Modern Language Association in Seattle in January 2020, I shared a question from the audience with the much larger online audience of the conference thread on *Twitter*. Letitia Henville, a Vancouver-based academic editor who holds a PhD in English from the University of Toronto, asked the panel, "[W]e've talked about digital humanities as method—is public humanities also a method?" Stacy Hartman, director of the Publics-Lab at the Graduate Center, City University of New York, who has a PhD in German studies from Stanford, instantly responded online. "It's a practice and a mindset," she wrote. "The best public work is conceived of as public from the very beginning. It is not simply 'translated' from academese. It serves multiple publics and purposes." In the background of this unfolding conversation, and while listening to the responses from the panel, I received another notification. Jim Cocola, associate professor of English at Worcester Polytechnic Institute and a contributor to this volume, had sent me an e-mail. He wasn't at the convention, but was following sessions remotely, and this question was one that he wanted to answer. "Public humanities are most certainly a method," he wrote, "a method that relies on thinking not only in but also with a public. Since thinking with one kind of public will yield different results than thinking with some other kind of public, the public humanities demand a carefully considered method indeed." Cocola's chapter in this volume elaborates on this idea and contextualizes it in the diverse public classrooms of the place- and text-based Bard College Clemente Course in the Humanities. It also indicates, to me, that rather than seek to develop a comprehensive methodological framework for the public humanities, each project plan will need to include time and space to carefully consider—to use Cocola's phrase—the terms of its engagement, the nuances of its public audience or partner, and the limits and possibilities of its work.

In the most "on the ground" versions of the public humanities—such as museums, state councils, and other nonprofit organizations with missions related to heritage, culture, and the interpretation of the arts—the methods under discussion at academic conferences like the MLA convention have already been integrated into daily operations. But these discussions among scholars within professional organizations and on campuses remain vitally important, not least because they have real consequences in the higher-education sector. How much work in the public humanities will be undertaken there? By whom? Under what conditions, and with what implications, for those who pursue it? In that same MLA convention session, panelists presented on new findings from a forthcoming study by analysts at the think tank Ithaka S+R, which were drawn from its Supporting Research in Languages and Literature project. Julie Frick Wade, associate editor of the *MLA International Bibliography with Full Text*, summarized the responses the project leads solicited from faculty at regional comprehensive colleges and universities. Many respondents, she noted, "are enthusiastic about public humanities—an orientation toward making humanities research accessible and valuable to the non-academic public" (Springer). But Frick Wade also noted that while many early career faculty reported a strong interest in pursuing public projects, they also described significant hesitation to invest time in that work before completing scholarly monographs and securing tenure.[3]

The hesitation among early career faculty to pursue public scholarship is likely based in an accurate sense of the departmental and institutional pressures bearing down on them.[4] At any level—individual, departmental, institutional—values and priorities are not always aligned. Put another way, work in public scholarship may be applauded but not rewarded. Pretenure professors in literary studies, and across the humanities, often have no clear path on which they might make contributions to their academic fields and to the public good—while being advanced in their careers for both. Furthermore, faculty of color confront this dilemma within the harsher context of what George Sanchez, professor of American studies and ethnicity and history at the University of Southern California, calls "a third faculty culture: one of professional ambivalence and bridge work between geographically close but socially distant communities of color; that is, the current culture for minority faculty at predominantly white universities." When faculty of color undertake work in public scholarship that is connected to "the commitments to communities of color almost all bring with them to the academy," he continues, the message that reverberates across academia and within departmental cultures is that they must "abandon those ties or risk professional suicide" (227). This impossible choice is one clear factor in what Patricia Matthew, associate professor of English at Montclair State University, describes as the "tenuous diversity" of academia (21). In her introduction to *Written/Unwritten: Diversity and the Hidden Truths of Tenure* (2016), she notes that new models are needed to assess the work of "faculty of color who might feel a different pull toward activism than their white counterparts" (20).

New models of scholarly assessment are needed; so, too, are new models of scholarly training.[5] It is evident that, two decades into the twenty-first century, "the entire system of knowledge generation is in flux," opening new possibilities alongside real challenges in higher education (Post 1). And, as

Margaret Post, Elaine Ward, Nicholas Longo, and John Saltmarsh powerfully argue in their collaboratively written opening pages of *Publicly Engaged Scholars: Next-Generation Engagement and the Future of Higher Education* (2016), entirely new frameworks for producing and authorizing knowledge are currently being built by emerging scholars, many of whom come from "what have been historically underrepresented populations—especially women, people of color, and low-income individuals—whose scholarly identities are tied more closely to community engagement" (4). They describe the ways in which the shift to public scholarship could transform higher education:

> These scholars act on their values through collaboration, inclusiveness, participation, task sharing, and reciprocity in public problem solving. Central to their approach is an authentic respect for the expertise and experience that everyone contributes to education, knowledge generation, and community building. Academic work is done with the public and is relational and localized even as it often has a global framework. Knowledge is cocreated and context-dependent with an emphasis on shared authority and ownership in its production. As a result, the university is part of an ecosystem of knowledge production addressing public problems with the purpose of advancing a more inclusive, deliberative democracy. (4)

What place might literary studies claim for itself in such a vision? How might its scholarly practices be reimagined by doing so? What new contributions could it make, in turn, to our understanding of the things that are, in the words of Toni Morrison, "hard, true, and lasting?" (224). The works collected in this volume provide a number of rich and vibrant answers. Looking out over the landscape of literary studies today, we can see that many other scholars in literary studies are working out their own responses to these same questions.

* * *

In the introduction to her groundbreaking 2019 book *Generous Thinking: A Radical Approach to Saving the University*, Kathleen Fitzpatrick, director of digital humanities and professor of English at Michigan State University, recounts a story. It is worth quoting in full:

> A few years ago, after a talk in which a well-respected scholar discussed the broadening possibilities that should be made available for humanities PhDs

to have productive and fulfilling careers outside the classroom, including in the public humanities, I overheard a senior academic say with some bemusement, "I take the point, but I don't think it works in all fields. There's long been a 'public history.' But can you imagine a 'public literary criticism?'" His interlocutor chortled bemusedly: *the very idea*. But the world has long been filled with public literary criticism, from the most well-regarded and widely disseminated book reviews through large-scale public reading projects to widespread fan production. All of these are modes of literary work that reach out to nonspecialist audiences and draw them into the kinds of interpretation and analysis that scholars profess, and we ignore that work to our great detriment. (35)

It is important to recall how pervasive public engagement has been, in various forms, throughout the history of the professionalized study of literature—much more so than is typically acknowledged or understood. There is, to take one example, the model of the English professor as public intellectual (in this frame of mind, one immediately thinks of a long list of distinguished thinkers whose public-facing writing has shaped discourses far beyond academia; to name a few: Michael Bérubé, Mark Edmundson, Stanley Fish, Henry Louis Gates Jr., Louis Menand, David Palumbo-Liu, Elaine Showalter, and Gayatri Spivak). These literary scholars write from their expertise for broad, if selective, public readerships. They use their specialized knowledge to broker meaningful engagements between texts and general readers that exceed the direct encounter of any given individual reading alone.

The website *Public Books* exemplifies this notion. It was founded in 2012 by Sharon Marcus, Orlando Harriman professor of English and comparative literature at Columbia University, in collaboration with anthropologist Caitlin Zaloom. It is frequently cited as the preeminent venue for public scholarship in literary studies. Its mission, summarized: "at *Public Books*, academics join with other public scholars, critics, and activists to make the life of the mind a public good." One might also think of a number of other publicly engaged websites that have a scholarly inflection: *Aeon, Brain Pickings, 5 Books*, and similar digital venues that have emerged as sites for essential humanities-based content in a digital age.

At its best, public engagement in literary studies can also be a form of advocacy for the humanities, persuasively making the case for the value of our work. As important are the texts that reflect that work and its public value back to its practitioners, with new insights for future commitments.

Doris Sommer's *The Work of Art in the World: Civic Agency and Public Humanities* (2014) and Helen Small's *The Value of the Humanities* (2013) are examples of books written by esteemed scholars in literary studies that have circulated widely in this way. And the stakes of the public perception of the humanities—in short, the general and always-changing sense among people from all walks of life, whose paths have never led them through the corridors of our departments, that our work has value *to them*—are high. In a foreword to the riveting new edited volume *Engaging the Age of Jane Austen* (2018), literary critic Teresa Mangum writes, "In a twenty-first-century context where the academic humanities are misunderstood, dismissed, and even derided, teachers of literature can hardly afford to confine their teaching to their classrooms. How, then, do we connect our immediate public—our students—and communities beyond our classrooms with the power that past literatures hold between their covers?" (xi). We need many more conversations centered on that very question and many more collections of exemplary work to persistently and concretely answer it.

* * *

This collection moves from examples of individual scholars reaching outward to larger publics to models of collaboration and cross-institutional partnership. Throughout, contributors reflect on the implications of public engagement for literary studies and, frequently, also discuss the stakes of not only the meaning and value of this work for individuals but ultimately also for long-term institutional change. All of the contributors to this volume embody a duality of professional commitments and roles, active both within the discipline and in public projects. Some of the chapters in this collection can be read as personal narratives, an important genre within discussions of the public humanities, in which the writer takes a long look back over many years of serious investment in public-facing work. By recognizing that many stories about the public humanities span full careers and draw upon decades of expertise in scholarly and public practice, we can see both the impressive level of commitment people bring to this work as well as the duration of its growth and its outcomes. Because public scholarship is so often based in relationships and reciprocity, it can take many years to yield its full results. At the same time, each essay or podcast episode released to a public audience—or, for example, each performance or exhibition, each community conversation—has its own distinct temporality and impact. Taken together, these chapters show the importance of each single engagement as well as their cumulative value over time. They also point the way forward, based on hard-won insights from years of experience and experimentation.

If scholars in literary studies are interested in reaching larger public audiences, and would primarily like to do so by reconceptualizing the most exciting insights from their research into a form of writing accessible to readers outside of the academy, where should they begin? Christopher Douglas, whose public-facing literary and film criticism on the intersection of religion and US politics has been shared online tens of thousands of times, shaping public discourse in deeply impactful—and viral—ways, shares his advice for successfully pitching and composing public-facing prose. His chapter illuminates the step-by-step process of publishing highly relevant, deeply informed critical analysis for online readerships in a digital age. While the pace of this publication process, and many of its specific demands, will be unfamiliar to those readers of this volume whose scholarship has appeared exclusively in traditional academic venues, what will be instantly recognizable to them is the content, method, and rigor of Douglas's work.

NEH public scholar Cynthia Haven, whose chapter demonstrates the incredible reach of her work, offers advice to scholars in literary studies who, like Douglas, want to think through the traditions of journalism in their turn to public scholarship. Haven's blog was one of the first digital literary venues of its kind, and she has undertaken important work in the early adoption of podcast technology as well. Her willingness to take risks in new mediums has been a defining aspect of her success, and her reflections on how scholars can remain consistently relevant while traversing a constantly changing media and communications landscape will have much to offer readers who are exploring possibilities for sharing their work on both established and emerging platforms.

Carmaletta Williams, whose research focuses on racial identity formation, writers of the Harlem Renaissance, the letters of Langston Hughes, and literature for children, is an Emmy–award winning performer of public-humanities narratives. In her chapter, she tells the story of how she came to win an Emmy for her role as Harlem Renaissance novelist, anthropologist, and folklorist Zora Neale Hurston on R. Crosby Kemper III's *Meet the Past* program on Kansas Public TV in 2015. The historical and biographical context through which she describes that crowning moment is inspiring: her public scholarship in literary studies has illuminated questions of racial identity formation for audiences in every corner of her home state of Kansas for decades and for students at the community college where she taught for a quarter of a century. Her insistence on the value of the humanities to the public shaped her professional career on and beyond her campus, and the strength of her convictions is its own form of advice for those who are considering whether or not they should invest their time—for all of us, time is a precious resource—into publicly engaged scholarship in literary studies.

In their collaboratively written chapter, Gary Handwerk, Anu Taranath, and Christine Chaney, all English faculty based in universities in Seattle, Washington, emphasize the nuts-and-bolts realities of sustaining humanities education partnerships across institutions over time. Their program, Texts and Teachers, a partnership with regional high schools offering dual-credit English courses for high school students, has been active, vibrant, and recursively productive for twenty years. They ask the fundamental question: What does it take to keep a program like ours alive? And they answer, in detail, that—more than budget lines or buy-in—relationships and shared values will always underwrite the long-term viability and success of partnership-based public-humanities programs. Their chapter includes notes on the program's infrastructure and ongoing operation, as well as its motivations and goals. Primarily, the chapter imparts to readers that cross-institutional partnerships, thoughtfully designed, have a real impact on student learning in literary studies—and on literary studies itself.

Jim Cocola, as associate professor and associate head in the Department of the Humanities at Worcester Polytechnic Institute (WPI) and academic director and poetry instructor in the local division of the Bard College Clemente Course in the Humanities, a program recognized internationally for bringing college-level humanities courses to people living in economic distress, writes on the challenges and the significant rewards—intellectual, interpersonal, societal—that come with this work. His chapter offers a nuanced articulation of the ways in which public engagement makes new insights for literary criticism possible—insights that would not be otherwise available to the field. It also points to a set of teaching practices for the literature classroom informed by an understanding of intersecting aspects of identity—such as race, class, gender, and sexuality—and positionality. Cocola's chapter details student engagement with a range of texts. Cocola imparts to readers a capacious sense of literary studies as a site of transformation, not only for teachers and individual students but also for the diverse publics of which they are a part.

The final chapter before my co-editor's concluding essay, like Cocola's, emphasizes the importance of honoring and trusting the knowledge of those who are positioned outside of institutions of higher education. Daniel Coleman and Lorraine York share reflections on their collaborative endeavors to establish a new Centre for Community Engaged Narrative Arts at McMaster University in Hamilton, Ontario, Canada. They reflect on how they approached this opportunity for institution building—namely, by drawing upon and honoring indigenous traditions, listening to and learning from community members before predetermining any aspect of the center's development, and leveraging grant-funded resources for community-led projects. The outcomes they describe are remarkable, and the takeaway advice they offer to readers can inform collaborative projects at any scale—particularly those in which community engagement is a key goal and value.

* * *

It is possible for us to overlook the quiet and persistent presence of scholarship in literary studies in public spaces. Take, for instance, the edited volume by literary critic Helen Vendler, *The Ocean, the Bird, and the Scholar: Essays on Poets and Poetry* (2015). Having traveled to a new town to attend a conference, and with an hour of time to myself, I casually walked through a local independent bookstore. Best sellers, genre fiction, journals, and glossy magazines vied for my attention. But there, on the eye-level shelf of an endcap display, was Vendler's book, the cover graced by beautiful seabirds in flight above darkened depths of water. I stopped, took the book in my hands. Any person in the store that day—anyone, that is, with access to resource-dense neighborhoods where brick-and-mortar bookstores still thrive—could have done the same. In an opening essay, Vendler writes movingly of the public value of the texts through which her own scholarship has found expression: poems. "Poetry belongs to all," she contends, but "its audience often needs—as I do still—paths into its inexhaustible precincts" (14). The acknowledgment of this need, shared by all readers, is the intellectual foundation of public scholarship in literary studies. We have brought this volume together to honor the work that is being done by faculty in English departments across the United States and Canada today to find and illuminate the paths into the inexhaustible precincts of literature with and for diverse publics. It is my conviction that this edited volume may indeed have a shaping role, alongside other statements and accounts of public scholarship, in the future of literary studies. The potential of this work is only beginning to be understood, and the public significance of literary studies has yet to be fully recognized. Our contributing writers offer us models through which we might reflect on our values and our commitments, and their work calls us to reconsider, and perhaps revise and strengthen, our own.

Notes

1. We recognize that the term *literary studies* is institutionally capacious and that it encompasses the work of faculty and graduate students in many other departments, especially those with a focus on language and literature. We have limited our inquiry to literary studies in English—setting aside also, as beyond our scope, the long traditions of public scholarship in composition and rhetoric, and the public contributions of creative writers—because, as coeditors, this is our shared area of expertise. It also was established as common ground among our contributors, most of whom initially submitted their chapters to us through a call for proposals to the membership of the Modern Language Association.

2. For imaginative analyses of what the total contributions of these graduates might be, see Laurence and Massing.

3. There are established and emerging guidelines for assessing public scholarship for the purposes of tenure and promotion. Examples include Ellison at al. and the Publicly Engaged Scholarship Criteria currently in use as a formalized process for the review and assessment of faculty work in this area at the University of Minnesota-Twin Cities (https://med.umn.edu/facultyaffairs/promotion-tenure/community-engaged-scholarship).

4. Furthermore, these conditions are distinct from those under which nontenure-track faculty do their work; adjuncts and full-time, nontenure-eligible instructors at colleges and universities face different challenges in pursuing public scholarship, including a lack of institutional investment and support and heavy teaching and service demands.

5. Much of the progress in this area has taken place at the level of graduate education. For further reading, and programmatic examples, see Bartha et al. (31–43); The PublicsLab at the Graduate Center, City University of New York; and the Public Humanities at Western University in Ontario, Canada, which, according to its website (https://www.uwo.ca/publichumanities/), "housed within the Faculty of Arts and Humanities, is a program designed to promote innovative forms of public scholarship, experiential learning, and community collaboration." And, programs at Georgetown and Iowa in the public humanities are under development and will soon launch; they were started with major stakeholder input from faculty and leadership in English at both institutions.

Works Cited

Bartha, Miriam. "Serious Work: Towards a Publicly Engaged Humanities." *Western Humanities Review*, vol. 64, no. 3, 2010, pp. 85–104.

Bartha, Miriam, and Bruce Burgett. "Why Public Scholarship Matters for Graduate Education." *Pedagogy*, vol. 15, no.1, 2015, pp. 31–43.
"Community Engagement." Social Sciences and Humanities Research Council, https://www.sshrc-crsh.gc.ca/society-societe/community-communite/index-eng.aspx. Accessed 5 Mar. 2021.
Ellison, J., and T. K. Eatman. *Scholarship in Public: Knowledge Creation and Tenure Policy in the Engaged University*. Imagining America, 2008.
Fitzpatrick, Kathleen. *Generous Thinking: A Radical Approach to Saving the University*. Johns Hopkins UP, 2019.
Graff, Gerald. *Professing Literature: An Institutional History*. U of Chicago P, 1987.
Laurence, David. "In Progress: The Idea of the Humanities Workforce." The Modern Language Association, 2009.
Lynch, Deidre Shauna. *Loving Literature: A Cultural History*. U of Chicago P, 2015.
Mangum, Teresa. "Foreword." *Engaging the Age of Jane Austen: Public Humanities in Practice*, edited by Bridget Draxler and Danielle Spratt, U of Iowa P, 2019, pp. xi–xiv.
Massing, Michael. "Are the Humanities History?" *New York Review of Books Daily*, 2 April 2019.
Matthew, Patricia. "Introduction: Written/Unwritten: The Gap between Theory and Practice." *Written/Unwritten: Diversity and the Hidden Truths of Tenure*, edited by Patricia Matthew, U of North Carolina P, 2016, pp. 1–25.
Morrison, Toni. "Hard, True, and Lasting." *The Source of Self-Regard: Selected Essays, Speeches, and Meditations*, edited by Toni Morrison, Alfred A. Knopf, 2019, pp. 220–26.
"National Foundation on the Arts and Humanities Act of 1965." National Endowment for the Humanities, https://www.neh.gov/about/history/national-foundation-arts-and-humanities-act-1965-pl-89-209. Accessed 5 Mar. 2021.
Ortiz, Ricardo L. "Introduction: Humanities as/and Comparatist Practice." *Post45*, 30 July 2019, https://post45.org/2019/07/introduction-public-humanities-as-and-comparatist-practice/.
Post, Margaret, et al. *Publicly Engaged Scholars: Next-Generation Engagement and the Future of Higher Education*. Stylus Publishing, 2016.
Sanchez, George. "Crossing Figueroa: The Tangled Web of Diversity and Democracy." *Collaborative Futures: Critical Reflections on Publicly Active Graduate Education*, edited by Amanda Gilvin et al., Syracuse UP, 2012, pp. 211–28.
Springer, Rebecca. "What Is Humanities Research Now? Roundtable at the Modern Language Association 2020 Convention." *Ithaka S+R Blog*, 14 January 2020, https://sr.ithaka.org/blog/what-is-humanities-research-now/.
Vendler, Helen. *The Ocean, the Bird, and the Scholar: Essays on Poets and Poetry*. Harvard UP, 2015.
Woodward, Kathleen. "The Future of the Humanities—in the Present & in Public," *Daedalus*, vol. 138, 2009, pp. 110–23.

Public Scholarship in the Age of the Christian Right

A Self-Interested Tale

Christopher Douglas

My first foray into public scholarship was motivated by brazen, shameless self-promotion. I had just published a book that seemed timely—*If God Meant to Interfere: American Literature and the Rise of the Christian Right* (2016)—and I wanted to promote the book to a potentially wider audience beyond English professors and other academics. In the book, I argued that since the 1970s, the unexpected political emergence of the Christian Right had been the crucial context, though sometimes an invisible one, for religiously interested US fiction of the last half century. The argument involved reading some novels that were obviously responding to Christian fundamentalism and its conservative politics, like Margaret Atwood's *The Handmaid's Tale* and Barbara Kingsolver's *The Poisonwood Bible*, but it also involved rereading other texts that spoke to the resurgence in roundabout ways and by indirect address— novels like Cormac McCarthy's *Blood Meridian*, Marilynne Robinson's *Gilead*, and even Dan Brown's *The Da Vinci Code*. The book seemed timely when it was published in the spring of 2016 during the election: the Christian Right didn't seem to be disappearing, as some prognosticators envisioned, and was slowly but resolutely coalescing around what seemed like an unlikely hero, Donald J. Trump.

My experience in trying to draw a wider audience's attention to my scholarly (but, I hoped, accessible) monograph provides some lessons for what literature scholars' roles can be when communicating with a broader reading public. These lessons include where to place material, how to shape writing for a nonacademic audience, techniques for framing literary analysis in terms of a broader "so what?" set of questions, and a rationale for why this might be important for us. "Public scholarship" is not a new phenomenon—academics have long written newspaper and magazine articles and "popular" books, done exposition on the Internet, and given talks to public audiences. For those of us teaching at public institutions receiving tax dollars from different levels of government, I think it's also a responsibility, part of our larger mandate, to communicate with the public and, as our granting agency in Canada puts it, effect "knowledge mobilization." But even if it isn't new, it's worth reviewing the practice and sharing the methods and strategies with others who are interested in speaking to a larger audience. In what follows, I concentrate on public writing for a general audience in online publications, though I have put some of the lessons drawn from this experience into the public lectures and discussions I've done over the last few years. This public writing is scholarly because it is research based. Of course, journalists do research as well for the purpose of investigation and reporting. What distinguishes public scholarship to my mind is that it is often work based on years of research into one's disciplinary field, most of which will not be communicated to the public. In this respect, think of public scholarship opportunities not as starting from scratch on a new research question but rather as shaping into a very small form an idea that you happen to know from your years of research experience.

Public scholarship is not just a matter of individual self-promotion. It can also be a matter of bringing hard-earned expertise to bear to counter widespread misunderstanding on the parts of the press and public. In our own era, a widespread religious illiteracy in society and in journalism manifests as incomprehension about how white evangelical Christians could support the irreligious pathological liar and serial adulterer Trump. Part of this incomprehension is due to the incorrect but simple assumption, even among the irreligious, that authentic and "real" Christianity couldn't possibly be authoritarian, racist, or unprincipled. Literature specialists are especially poised to comprehend and explain the four-century history of Christian white supremacy in the United States. The authoritarian will to power, its frequently violent expression, its unwillingness to share power or brook dissent—we who have read Frederick Douglass and Harriet Jacobs on slavery, or Richard Wright and James Baldwin on the church, or Mary

Rowlandson's fantasy of God's pedagogy, or read about the exile of Roger Williams, who contended that Puritan settlers needed to treat with Indigenous peoples—we know about the long reach and persistence of Christian white male supremacy. Responsible religious studies scholars can likewise contribute a critique of the popular but unearned wisdom that religion is naturally benevolent unless twisted by nonreligious outside forces. After four decades of white evangelical political resurgence, it has become clear that mainstream professional journalism—itself a profession under siege, which is part of the problem—lacks religious literacy in general. Journalists sometimes don't understand what religion is or how to write about it and some bring suppositions with them like the one previously mentioned, what we might call the pretense theory of religion (Douglas, *If God* 1–2), wherein religious expression, especially about power, is imagined as being "really" about something else. In this sense, journalism in the age of the Christian Right requires a supplement of publicly engaged scholarship because of the widespread misunderstanding about religion that is only just beginning to get addressed, as we've seen by the plethora of why-are-white-evangelicals-supporting-godless-Trump articles over the last four years. Doubtless there are other widespread unearned assumptions in other fields. Public-facing scholarship has public value.

In terms of practical counsel, my first piece of advice is to get used to rejection notices and silence. If you think publishing academic articles and books at journals and presses involves lots of rejection notices, steel yourself. There will be lots of nos from editors to pitches and pieces but, more than this, oftentimes just nonresponses from online magazines and established outlets. For a while, I kept a spreadsheet so I could track which outlets said no to which piece of public scholarship I'd sent or pitched, but after a year and a half, it just got too long and I abandoned it. My favorite rejection story is that a deceased editor at *The Times Literary Supplement* rose from the dead—twice—to reject two of my pitches, one on the friendship between Marilynne Robinson and Barack Obama and another on David Foster Wallace's depiction of evangelicals. (Obviously, someone at the paper was monitoring their late colleague's email address, but it was fun to think that my pitches were so awful that they called forth a dismayed repudiation even from the afterlife.) Fortunately, the rejections (or silences) from online outlets happen faster than in academic publishing cycles, giving authors a chance to shop ideas or essays faster.

The Occasion and the Pitch

My first attempt at public scholarship, a four-thousand-word essay on the creationism-evolution debates that were the context for Carl Sagan's composition of his science fiction classic *Contact*, was rejected by the online magazine *Religion Dispatches*. It was too long, its argument too detailed and complex—too reminiscent, in other words, of an academic journal article. But, intrigued by my take and the subject of my book, its editors proposed interviewing me about my book, using their "10Q" format of ten standard questions I answered. The resulting interview ("Untold") was in some sense my first foray into public scholarship.

The Sagan piece took another year to place, for a reason that provides another object lesson for publishing public scholarship: editors and outlets often want to know what the *occasion* for the pitched article is. Editors ask this question from the potential audience's point of view: when potential readers see the title of your piece on a homepage, or on social media, what will get the reader to click the link, read the piece, and hopefully share it with their networks? Why is the author talking about this idea, at this time? Journalists have to make pitches all the time. As figure 1 suggests, the *Conversation*—an excellent online publication tailored to academics trying to disseminate their research more broadly—invites authors to think about a potential piece in terms of "timely, evidence-based analysis of what's making the news" (https://theconversation.com/ca/pitches) (though other possibilities exist as well). I finally managed to get my Sagan piece published ("Contact") at *The Conversation* by following this advice and tying the analysis to the twentieth anniversary of the film version of *Contact*. As you can see if you read the piece, the "occasion" in this instance—the twentieth anniversary of the film version of a novel—is pretty flimsy, since the bulk of the article is actually about the conflict between science and religion in the novel, not the film. The lesson here is: be creative about what makes something timely or relevant. Anniversaries of publications or events, birthdays of authors, an older treatment of a theme that is relevant today, a film or television adaptation, a local performance (Douglas, "Darwin's"), and so on.

The Conversation knows what other newspaper editors and publishers know: readers often don't finish the entire article, so the most important material is placed first, followed immediately by the most important evidence, details, or context. *The Conversation* knows this because it measures how far readers scroll down its pages and, hence, whether they get to the

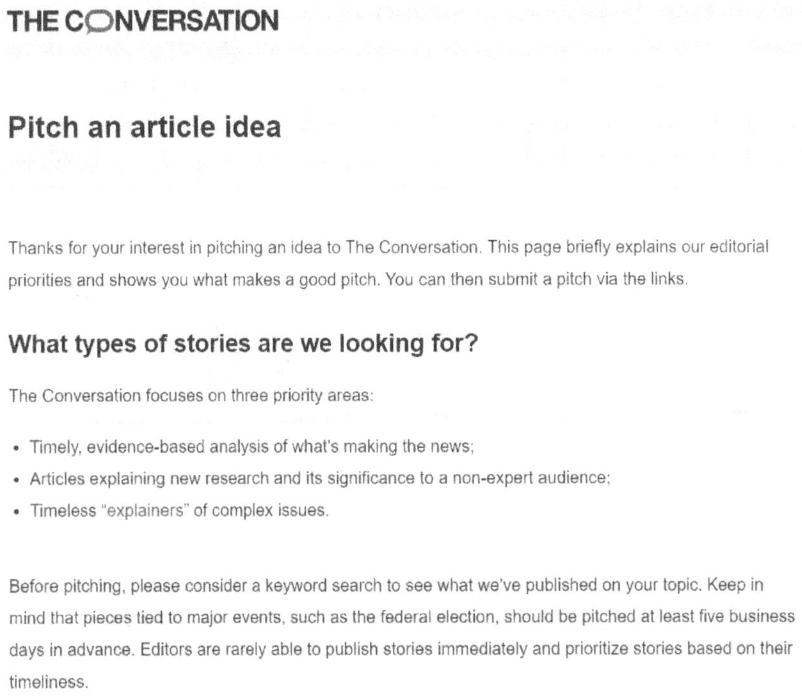

THE CONVERSATION

Pitch an article idea

Thanks for your interest in pitching an idea to The Conversation. This page briefly explains our editorial priorities and shows you what makes a good pitch. You can then submit a pitch via the links.

What types of stories are we looking for?

The Conversation focuses on three priority areas:

- Timely, evidence-based analysis of what's making the news;
- Articles explaining new research and its significance to a non-expert audience;
- Timeless "explainers" of complex issues.

Before pitching, please consider a keyword search to see what we've published on your topic. Keep in mind that pieces tied to major events, such as the federal election, should be pitched at least five business days in advance. Editors are rarely able to publish stories immediately and prioritize stories based on their timeliness.

Figure 1. The *Conversation*'s pitch page.

end of the articles. This Sagan piece was drastically shorter and reorganized compared to the four-thousand-word essay I tried to shop to *Religion Dispatches*. It was now just fourteen hundred words long, with many fewer details and a slimmed argument. What was particularly difficult for me to learn as I worked with the editors at *The Conversation* for this piece is that its model for academic journalism is the newspaper article, not the academic journal article.[1] An academic article often (1) frames a research question or problem, then (2) reviews previous scholarly treatments of the question, after which it (3) begins to provide detailed evidence leading to its (4) overall big idea and conclusion. But a newspaper article proceeds almost in the reverse way, beginning with the big idea or conclusion. This form of organizing one's ideas in argumentative writing was not easy for me, with my academic training, to learn to do. Fortunately, the editors worked with me to learn the new format as well as remove jargon and dense prose (as Sarah Bond counsels ["Vox"]). The result is a trade-off: this public scholarship on Sagan is simplified and shorter, but it's been viewed over twenty-three thousand times and shared on Facebook over twenty-three hundred times. In addition, *The Conversation* publishes its articles in an open-access model that allows free reproduction with attribution, and my Sagan piece was also run on the Web sites (but not print versions) of five local and national newspapers. The Conversation is a good place to start if you're thinking about pitching a piece of public scholarship (https://theconversation.com).

A third outlet I cultivated over time, *Marginalia*, which is a literature and religion "channel" of the *Los Angeles Review of Books*, has a slightly more academic tilt without the newspaper article organization of *The Conversation*. *Marginalia* prefers a sense of timeliness as well (though somewhat less), and so I had to think about the occasion for my article on the mutual admiration between Marilynne Robinson and Barack Obama, a kind of liberal Christian literary partnership we might think of in opposition to that of the Christian Right literary partnership of George W. Bush and *Left Behind* author Tim LaHaye. The occasion was relatively recent: the year before had witnessed the extraordinary literary event of a sitting president interviewing a living author, which had been published in a two-part *New York Review of Books* article in late 2015. I argued in the piece ("Literary") that Obama's and Robinson's literary politics laid in their shared romanticizing of Christian abolitionism, which was a little strange given that Robinson's most famous novel *Gilead* seems committed to forgetting Christian abolitionism's antagonist, proslavery Christianity.

Marginalia later published a piece that brings me to another lesson for literary critics looking to publish public scholarship: don't be afraid of popular, non-"serious" literature. I wrote a short essay on the way the bestselling evangelical novel *The Shack* had tried to rewrite the Biblical book of Job, with about as much success in explaining the problem of evil as the original Job ("Job"). Though *The Shack* piece might appear, and is sort of framed as, a *movie* review, the bulk of its "scholarship" content was actually an analysis of the complicated authorship of Job that the *novel* problematically revisited. Again, I used a film adaptation to finesse the question of the occasion for the piece. *The Shack* is a decidedly middlebrow evangelical bestseller but it has sold over twenty million copies worldwide, and it was made into a 2017 Hollywood movie featuring Sam Worthington and Octavia Spencer. Its influence, in other words, is far greater than the highbrow Christian-left writer of the present Marilynne Robinson, though not quite as great as the fundamentalist *Left Behind* series. It is academically sound to examine popular literature if we are trying to create a more complete literary history of religiously interested literature in the present. This is a lesson my Medievalist and Early Modern colleagues have taught me: if we are trying to draw an accurate map of the territory, as it were, we must include popular genres, low art beside high art. Fortunately, our attention to the popular can give us more occasions to bring our academic expertise to bear on a cultural history of the present in the form of public scholarship.

The Strange Things You've Accidentally Learned Are Opportunities for Public Scholarship

My most successful piece of public scholarship came from a historically adjacent topic to my main expertise as a literary historian: a piece on the religious "origins" of fake news. Part of my research into the Christian Right's presence in literature included investigating the wider history of twentieth-century fundamentalism in the United States and the way that fundamentalism had formed itself in reaction to two bodies of academic knowledge emerging from the nineteenth century: the science of biological evolution and the historical-critical method of Bible scholarship that explored the complex authorship, editing, transmission, and translation of the Bible. Fundamentalism rejects both these bodies of expert, academic knowledge, preferring instead an origin story of Adam and Eve in Eden and a notion of the Bible as a divinely inspired, indeed practically divinely authored, book that is without error or contradiction when properly understood. Building on these two constitutive moves, Christian fundamentalism in the United States created institutions of counter expertise to stand against these modern, secular accounts. Investigating the history and discourse of fundamentalism had given me—sort of accidentally and by the way—some insight into the larger frame of Christian Right epistemology in the United States (see figure 2).

Like many, I was stunned by the election in 2016 of an obvious con man and "bullshitter" (Frankfurt) as well as the role that "fake news" and "alternative facts" played in the post truth media environment where a foreign adversary was intervening, especially on social media, on behalf of one of the candidates and parties. I wrote a piece on the topic for *Religion Dispatches* called "The Religious Origins of Fake News and 'Alternative Facts.'"

Figure 2. My fifteen minutes.

In it, I hypothesized that the observed asymmetry in the consumption of fake news during the election—there seemed to be more of it targeted for, and shared by, political conservatives than liberals—could be traced back to the Christian Right's hostility to academic expertise and professional journalism. For decades, I contended, conservative white Christians had nurtured a skepticism toward these mainstream institutions that established and circulated expert knowledge. More, they had built a network of institutions of counter expertise: Bible colleges and universities, Christian publishers and bookstores, newspapers and magazines, radio and then television ministries, museums and campus clubs together formed a set of institutions that resisted elite, secular, expert knowledge. Religious conservatives had their own alternative information ecosystem that was, with its sister organizations in Republican propaganda organs such as Fox News, Breitbart, and Infowars, actively hostile to mainstream knowledge and which provided what the new president's advisor eventually called "alternative facts" (https://www.cnn.com/2017/01/22/politics/kellyanne-conway-alternative-facts/index.html). We should not have been surprised that the Christian Right's cognitive training of its members had resulted in an appetite for outrageous stories about the villainy (indeed, sometimes actual Satanism) of Hillary Clinton and the Democrats (Lopez, "Pizzagate").

The article in *Religion Dispatches* struck a nerve and was timely, and, importantly, it also led to other professional opportunities. It was picked up by some ex-evangelical thinkers and writers on social media, who recognized the closed epistemological bubble I was describing as that which they had escaped from, and they shared it with their much larger networks. Eventually, the article received seventeen thousand Facebook shares and hundreds or maybe thousands of tweets/retweets (its counters have since been reset). It was my fifteen minutes of Internet fame. Hofstra University invited me to speak on the topic during their annual Day of Dialogue in October 2017. Meanwhile, the Cambridge Institute on Religion & International Studies (CIRIS), which runs a policy network for European and North American diplomats on the subject of religion and international affairs, had recently polled its members for what their next topic for a research backgrounder should be. The diplomats responded that the role of fake news and religion was very much on everyone's minds. When the director of CIRIS reached out to a US academic center dedicated to studying media and religion for suggestions, its director in turn recommended my piece. CIRIS subsequently commissioned me to produce a background paper for its diplomatic network on the role that religion and fake news played in the 2016 US election but expanded to include what was also happening in several 2017 European elections. I subsequently discussed the already distributed background paper to a group of Western diplomats gathered at the Ministry of Foreign Affairs in Paris (though unfortunately only over Skype). This topic, um, stretched my area of expertise a significant distance from contemporary US fiction.

Don't Leave History to the Historians

I tell this story because it has a few lessons for those interested in public scholarship. First, public scholarship is not only, or primarily, about altruism and serving the public good. It is also, to go back to my opening line, about "brazen, shameless self-promotion." It can be all these things at once but it's best to recognize the self-promotion part. The second lesson here is that we literature scholars should not leave history to the historians. We all (probably) have periods of expertise, and those periods likely entail not just an extensive knowledge of the literary history of the period but also cultural history and its forms of mediation. I learned a lot about the theological, political, and social history of US fundamentalism, emergent since the late nineteenth century, when I was researching the origins of the Christian

Right so I could better understand the literary response to it. I had thus sort of accidentally achieved a kind of expertise about Christian Right history and epistemology, which went beyond (some versions of) strict literary criticism and attention to literary texts and language. (It also helped that I had myself once been a liberal Canadian version of the conservative American white evangelicals I was now studying and had taught at Furman University, a fairly conservative college in South Carolina whose student population was disproportionately white and evangelical.) Many of us know some cultural history, and we should not be afraid to use it for the purpose of public scholarship.

The third lesson from this experience of "fake news and religion" is the importance of promoting your own work on social media. For me, this means *Twitter* and *Facebook*. This should be done in conjunction with the outlet itself—you should retweet their tweet about your article, and you should get them to retweet your tweet about your article (obviously not at the same time, or even the same day). If you have published a book that is linked to the topic you've just published a piece of public scholarship on, ask your publisher to share your public scholarship on their social-media platforms. The same goes for your institution's media office. Does your department, faculty, and college use social media? Your colleagues? Ask them to share your work. Remember. Brazen. Self. Promotion. I especially direct this advice to younger scholars, women scholars, and minority scholars. Probably not enough people, or no one, is looking out for you. (For one instructive tale of a minority scholar's challenge in balancing public scholarship and community-engaged activist pedagogy in the years leading to her tenure review, see Few). As a white male, I've been socially trained to promote myself. (Over-)confidence is our thing; we invented the Dunning-Kruger effect. If you are a scholar and a woman and/or person of color, unlearn, to the extent that you can, lessons of silence, deference, humility, imposter syndrome. You belong, and your voice and expertise need to be heard. Some great women/minority public scholars whose work I follow closely on *Twitter* include Mary Dudziak, Jill Lepore, Nyasha Junior, Sarah E. Bond, Moudhy Al-Rashid, Jill Hicks-Keeton, Julie Ingersoll, Elaine Pagels, Andrea Jain, and Nathalie Maréchal.[2] Promote yourself and ask others to do so too. There will be times when institutional offices (and colleagues) politely decline, and that's fine. My public scholarship has an unavoidable political dimension to it that makes some institutions and people skittish; I respect their boundaries and do not unduly press them to help publicize my public scholarship. Your institution's community engagement, continuing education, and media-relations offices can also help you leverage your public and academic scholarship into community-oriented speaking engagements for local, nonacademic audiences—that is also public scholarship. This is their job, but as a public humanist, you're not as sexy as a climate scientist, so you have to ask them.

The fourth lesson I drew from this episode comes from the fact that the expanded report commissioned by CIRIS for its network of Western diplomats eventually became solicited by and then published in an academic journal, *The Review of Faith & International Affairs* ("Religion"). What had started as "public" scholarship had become regular academic scholarship. I think the lesson here is that the line between these modes is fuzzy, and working on writing for one audience can become writing for the other audience and vice versa.

This same lesson came home to me as I was trying, ultimately unsuccessfully, to write a piece for wider public consumption on David Foster Wallace's depiction of evangelicals in his quite amazing short story "Good People." In the story, which later became part of his unfinished novel *The Pale King*, a young white evangelical couple tries to figure out what to do about their unwanted pregnancy. In this rich depiction of psychological exploitation and self-deception, the focalizer eventually seems to abandon his manipulation of his girlfriend, whom he has sought to convince that God has seemingly blessed their decision to terminate the pregnancy. What was almost subversive about this sympathetic portrait of evangelicalism appearing in the liberal *New Yorker* in 2007, I argued, is that its readers would have had in mind a recent and spectacular example of evangelical (self-)deception and manipulation: the way the born-again George W. Bush had sold the Iraq War to the US public on the pretense of weapons of mass destruction and ties between Al-Qaeda and Saddam Hussein.

But explaining this larger context could not be ultimately reduced to the seven hundred- to two thousand-word range that often characterizes pieces of public scholarship. The resulting piece was eventually published in a peer-reviewed journal, but I convinced the journal, as a kind of "advertisement" for the special issue's topic of postsecularism, to make the article open access as its blog ("David"). While it is still accessibly written, mostly, it is now framed through an academic argument that the literary critical lens of thinking about recent religiously interested literature as *postsecular* is problematic because the latter term almost entirely dismisses what ended up being the major religious development of the last half century: the rise to political and social power of white evangelicals. In any case, this is an example of a piece of writing that began as an attempt at public scholarship that could not properly be developed as such and so changed into a more traditional (although still shorter) academic article.

You Have to Tell a Story

My public scholarship thus has fallen naturally into two categories: the Christian Right and literature and Christian Right epistemology. Both offer further lessons about how we might do literature-connected public scholarship. One problem we face is writing for a wide audience who may not know the literary text(s) that is the topic or occasion for the piece. How do we draw in readers unfamiliar with the text since we, like the editors to whom we're pitching the piece, want them to read the piece as well? I've found it useful to give a vigorous two- or three-paragraph plot summary of the novel in question, after an introduction that opens up the piece's key idea. In my piece on the way Philip Roth's *The Plot Against America* was not really a good "map" of the coming Christian fascism in the Trump era, it was necessary to explain in a little bit of detail the strange plot of *Plot* ("You've"). As a uchronia, or alternate history, Roth's novel imagines that the fascist sympathizer Charles Lindbergh runs against president Franklin D. Roosevelt in 1940 and wins. History changes course: Pearl Harbor doesn't occur; the Lindbergh administration reaches a diplomatic understanding with the Axis powers; and a renewed anti-Semitism begins to sweep the United States.

The plot synopsis became important not just because I wanted to draw in readers unfamiliar with the novel, but because the plotline was the location for a couple of authorial blind spots that were really the point of my essay. The threat of a Christian liberal fascism, as Roth imagines it in the novel, emerges as a set of government programs aimed at making America's Jews into better Americans, more assimilated to national life. But if the novel was about the rising evangelical Christian tide during the George W. Bush administration (as many reviewers thought), it gravely misunderstood the way evangelical expectations toward Jews are not motivated by the goal of making them more assimilated into the United States. Rather, it is to make Jews into Christians, to convert them—as the premillennial dispensationalism of evangelical theology holds will continue apace during the apocalyptic end-times, as depicted in Tim LaHaye and Jerry Jenkins's *Left Behind* series.

Plot synopsis is also one way of accomplishing what I think is a crucial component of public scholarship and academic journalism: you have to tell a story. In particular, I think it is important to offer a narrative and to construct the occasion for the piece around an "event." What happened or is happening? And why is it relevant, interesting, and important? In a pair of public-scholarship pieces on Hulu's adaptation of Margaret Atwood's *The Handmaid's Tale* for *Religion Dispatches*, for example, I did this on two levels. First was the level of plot synopsis: while many more people were probably engaged in the first season of Hulu's adaptation than were thinking about or reading *The Plot Against America* in 2017, I still wanted to enjoin readers who may not have read or seen the series. The story on this level is familiar to many but still enjoyable (in a manner of speaking) when retold: in a near-future United States struggling with an infertility epidemic, Christian theocrats mount a coup and establish a Christian dystopia wherein fertile women without political connections are forced to serve as "handmaids" for the supposedly infertile wives of the leaders, bearing children in their place. This plot can by summarized, but I am also talking about supplying a story on another level: what was *The Handmaid's Tale* as a cultural "event," a writerly intervention into the religious and political scenes when the novel was published in 1985, and when the adaptation emerged in 2017?

To describe *The Handmaid's Tale* as a cultural event is to tell the story of Atwood's contribution to the debates about women's reproductive rights that were a central part of the 1980s and, in particular, the growing power of the Christian Right's opposition to *Roe v. Wade*, such that it ended up in part "sorting" Republicans and Democrats into prolife and prochoice parties—and even, eventually, into making one party more religious and the other less. To tell this story is to provide the legal, political, and religious back history to the Christian prolife movement—another instance of not leaving history to the historians.

That story is generally recognized about Atwood's novel and its adaptation. What is less well known—and this is thus a third way of narrating the "event" of *The Handmaid's Tale*—is that Atwood was paying careful attention to not just the gender politics of the Christian Right but its racial history as well. Atwood's Gilead is not just a theocratic dystopia for many of its captive women—it is also a white Christian ethnostate whose racial justifi-

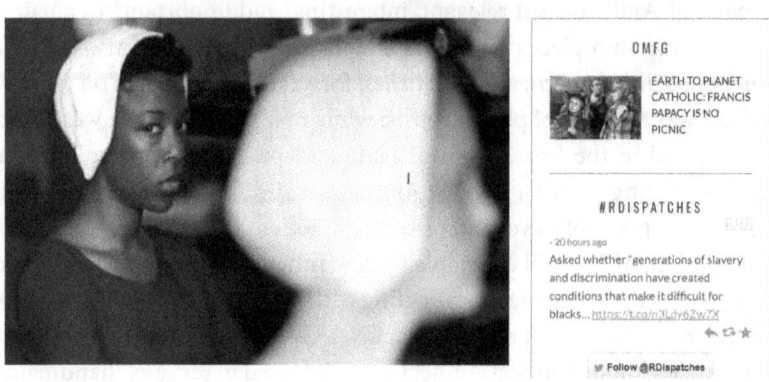

Figure 3. Not your parents' dystopian *Friends*.

cation reaches back to the theology and practice of Christian segregationism and Christian slavery before that. This is why the novel is saturated by African American enslavement narrative conventions, important intertexts for understanding the way that Gilead has modeled its practice of handmaid slavery on the African American slavery of the antebellum period. Atwood had done her homework, and the novel's 1985 critique of the contemporaneous Christian Right is that its theological and church-tradition ancestors were white evangelicals who believed in the God-given justification of white supremacy in the form of slavery before 1865 and Jim Crow segregation after that (see figure 3).

But my piece on *The Handmaid's Tale*, while rehearsing these stories, was really organized around narrating the event of the consequential change that Hulu's adaptation made to its source material in removing this aspect of the racial ethnostate that was part of Atwood's previous critique. For the admirable purpose of diversifying the cast, the producers made the narrator's best friend and husband African American characters. Otherwise, they were faced with building a television show around an all-white cast; it would have been like a dystopian *Friends*. But making this change, with Atwood's support, for the good reason of diversity had the consequence of eliminating the racial dimension of Atwood's critique of the Christian Right. I argued in the piece ("Why Hulu's") that the disappearance of this critique of the Christian Right's white supremacy was particularly disappointing in the Trump era, during which we have seen a reinvigoration of the white resentment and racism that some observers had imagined were the products of a bygone era. To narrate the event in this way is to explain the cultural consequence of an emergent artwork, which also answers an editor's key question about the timeliness of and occasion for a piece of public scholarship.

A companion piece on Hulu's adaptation had fewer narrative levels, beyond a similar short reiteration of a plot summary. The story I told took us back to the novel, and the event might be said to be an authorial blindness in imagining the Christian Right's rise to power as coming through violent revolution rather than a wholesale symbolic investment into the mythic apparatus of the United States. What I meant by that is that the Christian Right has generally sought to embrace and reimagine American identity: its history, institutions, and discourse. For all the brilliance of Atwood's novel, I argued that it missed the way the Christian Right has adopted and transformed the Republican Party and the United States. The Christian Right is authoritarian but repentance, return, and reformation mark its discourse—not revolution, for the most part—even if not all citizens are willing ("Why America's Handmaid's Tale," 2017). This piece thus narrates two events: the Christian Right's deliberate mobilization within US institutions in the twentieth century and the way Atwood's otherwise-incisive critique of this movement nonetheless misapprehended its methods and strategy. I am no longer confident in this argument in 2021, following years of conservative white Christian authoritarian voter suppression and antidemocratic agitation culminating in the failed January 6th insurrection.

When Public and Academic Scholarship Overlap

Narrating an event like an authorial blind spot, or an adaptation, or reviewers' misunderstanding a work—elements that make a piece of public scholarship timely—is likewise a way of solving what I suspect may be an obsta-

Figure 4. Social media as public scholarship.

cle to some academics considering public scholarship: the interface between one's academic, peer-reviewed publications and one's outward-facing academic journalism. Since there is ideally an overlap in content between these two areas, how does one handle the question of copyright and reprinting? How should we work with material that we've already published in an academic vein, and how do we publish in an academic outlet content we've already published in a more popular venue? Outlets often do not want to "reprint" a section of an already published academic book or article (except if you have a lot more fame than I do). Similarly, presses and journals may shy away from wanting to publish a peer-reviewed piece that expands a kernel that has appeared online (see figure 4).

The example of Kevin Kruse might help answer this question. A historian, Kruse works on the religious right in the United States and rose to some prominence when he published *One Nation Under God: How Corporate America Invented Christian America*. This book itself, while not quite public scholarship—it's got extensive footnotes and an index, etc.—is outward-facing and accessibly written for a larger audience. The book seemed to sell extremely well for an academic book (published by Basic Books), and in the years since its 2015 publication, Kruse has published public scholarship in online and print magazines and has a large (for an academic) social-media presence (four hundred and seventy thousand followers on *Twitter*, about four hundred and sixty-nine thousand more than me). Indeed, social media is also a particular site where Kruse's public scholarship takes place, in the form of *Twitter* threads on US religious and racial history. He has recently tangled several times, in long *Twitter* threads (@KevinMKruse) with conservative propagandist and dissembler Dinesh D'Souza who promotes the fake history that Republicans have been the (recent) party of civil rights. The issue for us, though, is the question of the overlap in subject and details between his published book and his online writing: if they aren't exact reprints, how are they not de facto excerpts ("Most"; "How")?

I think the answer here is that historical facts and the interpretation of them can't really be copyrighted, and while each piece of public scholarship may run over some of the same details and echo previous interpretations, it is also occasioned by different things and targeted toward different audiences. The same holds true with public scholarship emerging from literary criticism. The details of a piece of literature are not copyrighted except in the literature itself and can be paraphrased or quoted repeatedly in different contexts, for different occasions and audiences. For example, in my piece on the theologically difficult subject matter of Cormac McCarthy's famous *Blood Meridian*, I used the (again somewhat flimsy) occasion of the often-rumored-but-never-commencing film adaptation of the novel. The immediate "event" here was the difficulty in casting its vastly evil central antagonist Judge Holden for a film adaptation. But the more abstract "event" was how theology has struggled unsuccessfully to grapple with the problem of evil—both in terms of evolution but also in terms of a larger, almost one thousand-year set of theological developments among ancient Jews and Christians struggling to understand why the world could seem to be going wrong if it was governed by a single benevolent God. The piece thus told the story of the development of Jewish, and then Christian, apocalypticism in the ancient world—a hugely consequential theological development that continues to animate the moral dualism of the Christian Right—and then the even stranger, upside-down world of ancient gnosticism, which came to the not unreasonable conclusion that God might not be so good after all. This is a huge story that can only be briefly summarized in a piece of public scholarship. My piece in *The Conversation* (see figure 5) argued that it was actually these very strange and disturbing theological trends that ultimately would make the novel uncastable and probably unfilmable ("Unfilmable").

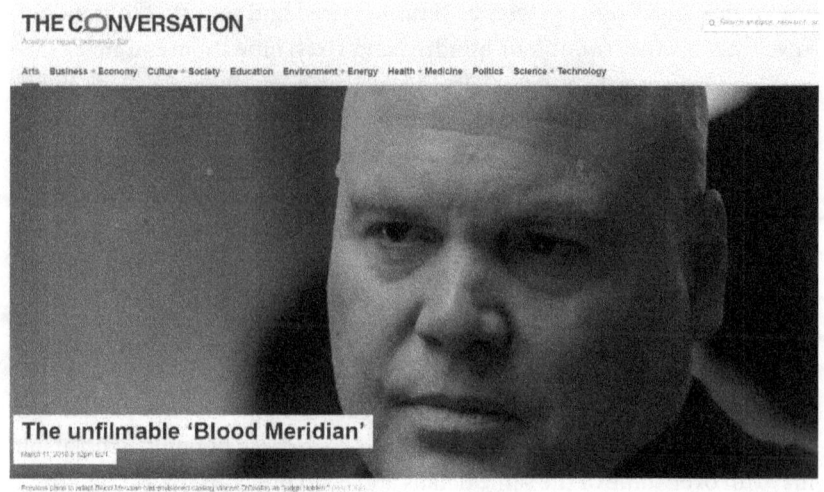

Figure 5. Occasion, copyright, reprinting.

This take echoed some of the details and argument in my book *If God Meant to Interfere*. But, analogous to Kruse's public work, it discussed established historical developments—twentieth-century theology grappling with evolution, ancient theology grappling with a world gone wrong—that are not copyrightable. In addition, it reframed these questions as they pertain to the novel by the occasion of the lack of progress on its film adaptation. Readers of Kruse's book and public scholarship will find significant overlap of historical facts and ideas—the latter in a much less detailed way, without an academic apparatus. I think of my sometimes-overlapping work in the same way. We're not reprinting (our own) copyrighted material, though we are running over some of the same ground in new contexts and occasions for different audiences. A similar situation held for my piece responding to Kurt Andersen's excerpt in the *Atlantic* from his book *Fantasyland: How America Went Haywire—A 500-Year History*, where he attributed America's current post-truth madness to the influence of new age hippies and academic postmodernism. Responding in *Religion Dispatches*, I argued that there was little evidence of conservative thought leaders ever reading, let alone adopting, academic postmodernism, but there was a lot of evidence that the Christian Right's particular epistemology accounted for much of the hostility to the "reality-based community" that Andersen was describing ("How"). (Andersen later responded to me on *Twitter* that *The*

Atlantic excerpt was actually the exception in the book that paid much more attention to religious influences [@KBAndersen].) This piece rehearsed some of the historical facts and ideas from my book, now repurposed for the occasion of a critical review of Andersen's think piece, but it did not reprint copyrighted material. In the one instance in which I repeated a specific idea—that we actually did witness in the twentieth century the development of a "Christian postmodernism"—I duly gave attribution to the book itself.

Keeping this distinction between academic publication and public scholarship in mind, the latter can be used to publicize the former, especially in tandem with a social-media presence. For example, I published a long and detailed article in the *Journal of the American Academy of Religion* arguing that in the evangelical bestseller *The Shack*, its author, William Paul Young, had inadvertently rediscovered the ancient Israelite polytheism of three thousand years ago for the simple reason that justifying the gods' ways to humans is an easier task than justifying God's ways to humans. Timed for its release, I wrote a companion article for the *Conversation* that tried to distill the argument of the seventeen-thousand-word academic article into a one-thousand-word public scholarship publicity piece for it—he same general argument in much less detail for different audiences ("Popular"). The journal and its editor supported this additional publicity, making the article open access for a time. I engineered a similar arrangement when I wrote a public-facing piece about a special issue of *Christianity & Literature* I had guest edited on "Literature of/about the Christian Right" ("Fundamentalist") and then used social media to highlight the special issue, with a brief synopsis of each contributor article (Douglas, "In").

These examples bring me to a final point about literary studies as public scholarship: the advantage of online publications and social media for public scholarship is that they allow extensive use of images, a luxury not often available for academic publications on literary studies. So, my *Conversation* piece on ancient Israelite polytheism in *The Shack* allowed for the incorporation of several striking images of statues of ancient Near East deities. I publicized the *Conversation* article in turn with a *Twitter* thread that featured even more images (Douglas, "I wrote"). This thread was a thread-of-threads because I had seeded, the month before, a series of threads on Canaanite mythology. So, in my thread-of-threads, I was able to point back to the Canaanite stories found on the clay tablets discovered at the lost city of Ugarit: the unlucky human heroes Kirta and Aqhat, and the storm god

Baal's victorious struggle over Sea, only to be defeated by Death.[3] I would argue that these tweet threads are instances of using social media to do public literary studies: not just in pointing to *The Conversation* article, which is also a form of literary studies, but the tweets themselves telling stories, using images, making comparisons for the wider public.

On Not Getting Paid: The Economics of Public Scholarship

As a way of concluding, I'd like to offer a final thought on another issue linked to questions of economics, copyright, and authorship. Namely, that when tenured scholars do public scholarship and academic journalism, we may be doing work that freelancers need and need to get paid for. If one is (as I am) a tenure-track, reasonably well-paid academic laborer without the precarity of underemployed/sessional/adjunct status, we may be doing for free the job that other professionals need to get paid for. (I've never been paid for any public scholarship I've done and do not expect to be, though I did get reimbursed when CIRIS commissioned me to produce the report for its diplomatic network.) I discussed this question with one freelance journalist, and we agreed that at least one answer to this question is an outlet like *The Conversation*, which is organized for academics trying to broaden their audience, which never pays its contributors, and which is never compensated by other outlets that reprint its content. I think, therefore, that my two pieces appearing there on the religious implications of the film adaptations of *Contact* and *Blood Meridian* are unlikely to have taken away compensated labor from an underpaid freelance journalist. Conversely, my friend Chrissy Stroop (https://cstroop.com/), an underemployed academic specializing in Russian history, gender, and evangelical politics, is in a different situation—being paid by several outlets for what I would call public scholarship and who may be transitioning to an alternative-academic career of academic journalism, public speaking, and advocacy.

Chrissy has become a very important voice in public scholarship on evangelicalism, but she has been pushed to do so by the profound crisis in our profession of the adjunctification of academic labor. Perhaps if more tenure-track scholars engaged in public-facing work, it could be part of a more robust defense of the need for tenure-track humanists instead of the economically exploitative sessional labor pool. Conversely, public scholarship may be an activity that younger scholars just finishing or who have finished their dissertation should not concentrate on: public scholarship cannot replace the value of academic scholarship during a job search. There is good counter pressure at the moment in favor of counting this kind of work toward tenure (see, for instance, Ellison and Eatman's important report Scholarship in Public), but institutions are conservative, and one can't currently count on enlightened policies. While passing through editorial processes, sometimes quite rigorous ones, online public scholarship is not peer reviewed. My advice for younger scholars would be that if an opportunity arises that will not take too much time and energy away from an academic publication, take it. It is also easier to do public scholarship—especially of a political kind, as mine is—from the safety of tenure.

My second answer to this question of economics is that public scholars bring to the table a kind of deep context that is unusual for mainstream and freelance journalists. This deep context comes from our disciplinary expertise and is the reason that, while we academics can often only speak with authority about a fairly narrow range of things, we are not starting from scratch when we write public scholarship. Having spent years on a few subjects, we know them deeply in a way most journalists don't have time to develop. We can also hear the ways our subjects resonate with current events and know the old answers to what can seem like strange and new paradoxes. For example, noticing that public discourse seemed to be full of examples of commentators trying to call out the hypocrisy of Christian Right and Republican leaders for purporting to have certain values one year and then abandoning them when convenient, I wrote a piece for *Religion Dispatches* explaining that the reason the critique of hypocrisy no longer worked is that it had never worked. The target of hypocrisy critique was not the audience for hypocrisy critique ("Why Has"). It hadn't been for the master critic of hypocrisy, Jesus, and nor had it been for what might be considered the more proximate context for our questions of Christian Right bad faith, which is the history of Christian slavery, its antecedent. Indeed, one of the most powerful literary critiques of Christian hypocrisy in the American scene had been Frederick Douglass's indictment of Christian enslavers in his *Narrative of the Life of a Slave*. His critique of the hypocrisy of enslavers, I pointed out, would never have convinced any of his ethical targets—but it was probably not meant for them. I would suggest that my strategy of invoking this famous literary charge of hypocrisy—Douglass on Christian slavery—in an analysis of the bad faith of the contemporary Christian

Right, is an unusual piece of context and a rare lens that is unlikely to have cost the livelihood of independent, freelance journalists. (There would certainly be exceptions to this rule.)

I brought a similarly unusual context to bear on the question "Can Christians Lie?," a piece occasioned by the striking ability of White House spokesperson and evangelical Christian Sarah Huckabee Sanders to dissemble ("Can"). The frame of intention and sincerity was too simple to really capture the challenge posed to our institutions by the deceptions and bad faith of Sanders and the Christian Right she comes from, I argued. The deeper function of Christian Right epistemology reaches back to questions not just of fundamentalist Bible reading practices like "harmonization" but also the conservative white evangelical hostility to mainstream expertise that has been developing for over a century. This wider framing of the question of deception in terms of the epistemic crisis that characterizes US religious conservatism today, while not unique, is an unusual historical contextualization of the way in which the Trump administration lied about its policy of separating children from their refugee parents at the border. Performing this kind of analysis, I think, probably does not take away the opportunity for freelancers to earn wages for work too often. If my public scholarship "beat" is the Christian Right, it will be rare to find a journalist who duplicates my two angles of literature and epistemology. Such as it is, it's this idiosyncratic mix that I can bring to the table. You probably have a similarly rare mix of interests and expertise. What is it?

Public scholarship won't save literary studies or humanities and solve their various crises. But it can be part of a broader move to demonstrate the value of the humanities to a wider public, a way of gaining trust but also responding to our mandates as publicly supported institutions of learning. Through civic engagement and communication, public scholarship has a role to play in strengthening democracy and promoting the public good, as Nicholas Behm, Sherry Rankins-Robertson, and Duane Roen argue ("Case").[4] Public scholarship can encourage wider audiences to consider themselves as stakeholders of what we humanists do. One audience member in a STEM-related profession came up to me after one public lecture and expressed surprise at my use of the word *research* to describe my investigation into how literature was responding to the age of the Christian Right. If the public is not used to thinking of literary studies and literary history as a kind of research activity—let alone a useful one that illuminates the deepest questions of who we are and how we should live—public scholarship can help advance our discipline's visibility and reputation. This is no less true for colleagues in other fields across our campuses who may believe that we "just read books" but learn otherwise when they stumble upon our public scholarship, as they may be more likely to do than come across our publications aimed at a disciplinary academic audience.

Notes

1. Although "academic journalism" has no greater a fixed meaning than "public scholarship," perhaps the former connotes even more the aspects of reporting, narrative storytelling, and timeliness.

2. All of these public scholars can be found online: Mary Dudziak, https://www.marydudziak.com/; Jill Lepore, https://scholar.harvard.edu/jlepore/home; Nyasha Junior, https://twitter.com/NyashaJunior; Sarah E. Bond, https://www.insidehighered.com/blogs/gradhacker/take-your-scholarship-public; Moudhy Al-Rashid, https://twitter.com/Moudhy; Jill Hicks Keeton, http://jillhickskeeton.oucreate.com/public-scholarship-and-online-essays/; Julie Ingersoll, https://twitter.com/julieingersoll; Elaine Pagels, https://www.elaine-pagels.com/; Andrea Jain, https://twitter.com/andrearjain; and Nathalie Maréchal, https://nathaliemarechal.net/.

3. For my explanation of this story, see these relevant *Twitter* threads: Kirta, https://twitter.com/crddouglas/status/1250570138946088961?s=20; Aqhat, https://twitter.com/crddouglas/status/1250901531370684417?s=20; the Sea, https://twitter.com/crddouglas/status/1251295397747871744?s=20; and Death, https://twitter.com/crddouglas/status/1251651721824292864?s=20.

4. That said, their article is a symptom of the polite academic neutrality that condemns political obstructionism and cynical "political theater" but is unwilling to name the fundamental asymmetry of the situation, marked in particular by the Christian Right-controlled Republican Party's intransigence and the conservative epistemic crisis (Roberts, https://www.vox.com/policy-and-politics/2017/11/2/16588964/america-epistemic-crisis). There is a partisan reason that academics are unable "to make their research on critical topics, such as climate change and evolution, understandable to lay audiences"—one that goes to the heart of the political rise of the Christian Right. As the bipartisan team of Mann and Ornstein (https://www.washingtonpost.com/opinions/lets-just-say-it-the-republicans-are-the-problem/2012/04/27/gIQAxCVUlT_story.html) explained,

> However awkward it may be for the traditional press and nonpartisan analysts to acknowledge, the Republican Party has become an insurgent outlier—ideologically extreme; contemptuous of the inherited social and economic policy regime; scornful of compromise; unpersuaded by conventional understanding of facts, evidence and science; and dismissive of the legitimacy of its political opposition. When one party moves this far from the center of American politics, it is extremely difficult to enact policies responsive to the country's most pressing challenges.

If public scholarship is to complement professional journalism's mission to prevent democracy from dying in darkness, it must be able to name this aspect of the problem (https://www.washingtonpost.com/lifestyle/style/the-washington-posts-new-slogan-turns-out-to-be-an-old-saying/2017/02/23/cb199cda-fa02-11e6-be05-1a3817ac21a5_story.html).

Works Cited

Andersen, Kurt (@KBAndersen). "Yes, extreme Protestantism a vastly more important source of our epistemological crisis than campus relativism—as I explain in Fantasyland." *Twitter*, 10 Aug. 2017, 1:54 p.m., https://twitter.com/KBAndersen/status/895750134222528512?s=20.

Behm, Nicholas, Sherry Rankins-Robertson, and Duane Roen. "The Case for Academics as Public Intellectuals." American Association of University Professors, Jan.–Feb. 2014, https://www.aaup.org/article/case-academics-public-intellectuals.

Bond, Sarah. "Vox Populi: Tips for Academics Transitioning to Public Scholarship." *Forbes*, 31 Jan. 2018. www.forbes.com/sites/drsarahbond/2018/01/31/vox-populi-tips-for-academics-transitioning-to-public-scholarship/#66a0da0d1a60.

Douglas, Christopher. "Can Christians Lie?" *Religion Dispatches*, 29 June 2018, https://rewire.news/religion-dispatches/2018/06/29/can-christians-lie-fundamentalist-bible-interpretation-shaped-truth/.

———. "'Contact' and Carl Sagan's Faith." *The Conversation*, 10 Nov. 2017, https://theconversation.com/contact-and-carl-sagans-faith-85150.

———. "Darwin's Sacred Song: Dan Brown's Brother Wrote a Sacred Mass about Charles Darwin." *Marginalia*, 11 January 2019, https://marginalia.lareviewofbooks.org/darwins-sacred-song/.

———. "David Foster Wallace's Evangelicals: The Other Postsecularism." *Christianity & Literature*, vol 67, no. 3, 548–58, christianityandliteratureblog.com/blog-1/2018/6/2/david-foster-wallaces-evangelicals-the-other-postsecularism. Accessed 11 Aug. 2020.

———. "How America Really Lost Its Mind: Hint, It Wasn't Entirely the Fault of Hippie New Agers and Postmodern Academics." *Religion Dispatches*, 9 Aug. 2017, https://religiondispatches.org/how-america-really-lost-its-mind-hint-it-wasnt-entirely-the-fault-of-hippie-new-agers-and-postmodern-academics/.

———. *If God Meant to Interfere: American Literature and the Rise of the Christian Right*. Cornell UP, 2016.

———. "In a new piece for @RDispatches, I argue we should read fundamentalist fictions as a way to understand 'the scandal of the evangelical mind.' Evangelical identity and knowledge circulate through storytelling—as with all other human groups. @SSHRC_CRSH /1." *Twitter*, 2 April, 3:02 p.m., https://twitter.com/crddouglas/status/1245833991279669248?s=20.

———. "Introduction to 'Literature of / about the Christian Right.'" *Christianity & Literature*, vol. 69, no. 1, 2020, pp. 1–14. *Project MUSE*, muse.jhu.edu/article/752345.

———— (@crddouglas). "I wrote a weird piece for @ConversationCA on the evangelical bestseller The Shack, arguing that it tries to solve the problem of evil by discovering . . . ancient Israelite polytheism. /1." *Twitter*, 13 May, 4:40 p.m., https://twitter.com/crddouglas/status/1261078962824007684?s=20.

———. "Job on the Big Screen: How The Shack Rewrote Scripture." *Marginalia*, 17 Mar. 2017, http://marginalia.lareviewofbooks.org/job-big-screen/.

———. "The Literary Politics of the Christian Left." *Marginalia*, 29 Aug. 2016, http://marginalia.lareviewofbooks.org/literary-politics-christian-left-christopher-douglas/.

———. "Popular Christian Novel *The Shack* Finds a Surprising Solution to the Problem of Evil: Polytheism." *The Conversation*, 14 May 2020, https://theconversation.com/popular-christian-novel-the-shack-finds-a-surprising-solution-to-the-problem-of-evil-polytheism-135668.

———. "Religion and Fake News: Faith-Based Alternative Information Ecosystems in the US and Europe." *The Review of Faith & International Affairs*, Mar. 2018, pp. 61–73.

———. "The Religious Origins of Fake News and 'Alternative Facts.'" *Religion Dispatches*, 23 Feb. 2017, https://religiondispatches.org/the-religious-origins-of-fake-news-and-alternative-facts/.

———. "This Is *The Shack* That Job Built: Theodicy and Polytheism in William Paul Young's Evangelical Bestseller." *Journal of the American Academy of Religion*, vol. 88, no. 2, June 2020, pp. 505–42, https://doi.org/10.1093/jaarel/lfaa021.

———. "The Unfilmable *Blood Meridian*." *The Conversation*, 11 Mar. 2018, https://theconversation.com/the-unfilmable-blood-meridian-91719.

———. "An Untold Tale: American Fiction vs. the Religious Right." *Religion Dispatches*, 8 Jun. 2016, https://religiondispatches.org/who-are-we-and-how-should-we-live-american-literature-and-the-god-gap/.

———. "What Fundamentalist Christian Fiction Can Teach Us About Our American Crisis." *Religion Dispatches*, 2 Apr 2020, https://religiondispatches.org/fundamentalist-fiction-provides-a-window-into-the-evangelical-apocalyptic-worldview-thats-helped-bring-us-to-our-current-crisis/.

———. "Why America's Handmaid's Tale Doesn't Look Like Hulu's." *Religion Dispatches*, 15 Jun 2017, https://religiondispatches.org/why-americas-handmaids-tale-doesnt-look-like-hulus/.

———. "Why Has the Critique of Hypocrisy Run Out of Steam?" *Religion Dispatches*, 14 May 2018, https://religiondispatches.org/why-has-the-critique-of-hypocrisy-run-out-of-steam/.

———. "Why Hulu's 'Handmaid's Tale' May Be the Wrong Adaptation for Trump Era." *Religion Dispatches*, 25 Apr. 2017, https://religiondispatches.org/why-hulus-handmaids-tale-may-be-the-wrong-adaptation-for-trump-era/.

———. "You've Been Warned: Reading Philip Roth's *The Plot Against America* in the Trump Era." *Religion Dispatches*, 18 Sep. 2017, https://religiondispatches.org/youve-been-warned-reading-philip-roths-the-plot-against-america-in-the-trump-era/.

Ellison, Julie, and Timothy K. Eatman. "Scholarship in Public: Knowledge Creation and Tenure Policy in the Engaged University." *Imagining America: Artists and Scholars in Public Life Tenure Team Initiative on Public Scholarship*, 2008, https://community-wealth.org/sites/clone.community-wealth.org/files/downloads/paper-ellison-eastman.pdf.

Few, April L., et al. "Balancing the Passion for Activism with the Demands of Tenure: One Professional's Story from Three Perspectives." *NWSA Journal*, vol. 19, no. 3, 2007, pp. 47–66. *Project MUSE*, muse.jhu.edu/article/224747.

Frankfurt, Harry. "On Bullshit." *Princeton University*, www2.csudh.edu/ccauthen/576f12/frankfurt__harry_-_on_bullshit.pdf. Accessed 11 Aug. 2020.

Kruse, Kevin (@KevinMKruse). "Ask and ye shall receive." *Twitter*, 31 Jul. 2018, 11:27 a.m., https://twitter.com/KevinMKruse/status/1024360878760779776?s=20.

———. "How Corporate America Invented Christian America." *Politico Magazine*, 16 Apr. 2016, https://www.politico.com/magazine/story/2015/04/corporate-america-invented-religious-right-conservative-roosevelt-princeton-117030.

———. "The Most Successful First 100 Days Of An Administration Didn't Belong to Who You (or Donald Trump) Think." *Esquire*, 27 Apr. 2017, https://www.esquire.com/news-politics/news/a54732/ike-100-days/.

———. *One Nation Under God: How Corporate America Invented Christian America*. Basic Books, 2015.

Lopez, German. "Pizzagate, the Fake News Conspiracy Theory That Led a Gunman to DC's Comet Ping Pong Explained." *Vox*, 8 Dec. 2016, https://www.vox.com/policy-and-politics/2016/12/5/13842258/pizzagate-comet-ping-pong-fake-news.

Mann, Thomas E., and Norman J. Ornstein. *It's Even Worse Than It Looks: How the American Constitutional System Collided with the New Politics of Extremism*. Basic Books, 2012.

Roberts, David. "America Is Facing an Epistemic Crisis." *Vox*, 2 Nov. 2017, https://www.vox.com/policy-and-politics/2017/11/2/16588964/america-epistemic-crisis.

Wallace, David Foster. "Good People." *The New Yorker*, 5 Feb. 2007, https://www.newyorker.com/magazine/2007/02/05/good-people.

What Lasts

Cynthia L. Haven

I have been called the "public face of literature at Stanford," yet my field was originally journalism. I began the time-honored way for that profession, via the newsroom rather than academia, first with newspaper articles and, eventually, with magazines, Web sites, and academic journals. I eventually produced a shelf of books on Nobel poets Joseph Brodsky, Czesław Miłosz, and other British and US poets; I even coauthored a book with the Stanford University president. More recently, my 2018 biography, *Evolution of Desire: A Life of René Girard*, received widespread international acclaim. It was lauded in *The New York Review of Books* and discussed on the floor of the prestigious Académie Française. I am a National Endowment for the Humanities public scholar. However, I play two roles: in addition to my work as an author and journalist, I also advance, advocate, and participate in humanities outreach for Stanford University.

My adventures with "public scholarship" began when I became the arts and humanities writer at Stanford in 2007. My work put me in touch with the thinkers and writers who would change my life—French theorist René Girard, his fellow academician Michael Serres, Milton scholar Martin Evans, Dostoevsky biographer Joseph Frank, historian and poet Robert Conquest. In 2011, I conducted the only video interview of Serres speaking in English, available at https://www.youtube.com/watch?v=zb5-l45dbow&t=9s. Within a few years, the world moved into warp drive, and so did I. In the news media, everything became faster, shorter, and often more trivial, as millions have sought to cram meaning into one or two hundred characters. I came in on the ground floor and learned to leverage my influence with Facebook, Twitter, and other platforms.

The task of making the case for literature, and the humanities more generally, has never been more urgent. Great literature is endless. Nevertheless, it has become the province of a shrinking coterie who prefer solitary insight to Snapchat, something with a metaphysical bite rather than bytes. *Quo vadis?* Some years ago, the Polish poet Adam Zagajewski outlined one option for the future during our interview: "We'll be living in small ghettos, far from where celebrities dwell, and yet in every generation there will be a new delivery of minds that will love long and slow thoughts and books and poetry and music, so that these rather pleasant ghettos will never perish—and one day may even stir more excitement than we're used to now" (Haven, "Only"). It may come to that. I'll opt for a less exclusive option: we may still learn to make a persuasive case for literature to a wider public, opening the essential world of literature across lines of class, race, and ethnicity.

A Community of the Like-Minded: Social Media

It's been said that the reason people have children today is to raise their own IT departments. It's a practical consequence of child rearing, but you don't have to be young to "get it," and you don't have to be up to date with every new innovation to reap substantial professional benefits from social media. In fact, using one or two platforms very effectively is probably more advantageous than dispersing your energies on half a dozen that never catch fire. You have to define what "success" is, in a way that aligns with your aims.

Nobody begins as an "expert"—and no one ever learns everything. There's too much to know, and it changes daily. The good news is that you don't have to know everything to be effective. Take heart: I, too, am entirely self-taught. Although I got serendipitous help and guidance along the way, I was pretty much on my own.

First lesson: we all have to build our audience and our numbers. Eventually, I reached far more readers than I ever expected—but I started from scratch with a handful of *Twitter* followers and no understanding of what I needed to do to build a "platform." I learned that too often newcomers see social media— whether a blog or a tweet— as a sort of billboard or a personal diary. In short, merely as a way of getting the word out on your terms. However, to enter each social medium is to join a community or, rather, to create a community of the like-minded, tailored to your interests, your sensibility, your obsessions. You learn to give and receive help, first online and soon offline. You help each other out with a retweet or a useful tip or a reference or a Facebook comment or whatever you can give. You will celebrate each others' victories and console each other in defeat. I didn't know that yet, but I began to get an inkling when the Stanford press release announcement for my new blog *The Book Haven* went out ("The Book Haven": see also Ray) and Frank Wilson, the retired *Philadelphia Inquirer* book editor who runs the high-traffic *Books Inq.* blog, emailed me to offer his support. (Nota bene: you do not launch a blog with a press release; its recipients occupy a different planet.) I would "meet" others online—Abbas Raza and Morgan Meis of the phenomenal *3QuarksDaily*; Patrick Kurp of the polished and rigorously daily *Anecdotal Evidence*; Rhys Tranter's lively *Rhys-Tranter.com* on literature, philosophy, and the arts; Don Selby of the highly influential *Poetry Daily*. In cyberspace, too, you can cross the nigh impassable barrier of time—forging alliances with people across generations as well as across the world. Important for both ends of the age spectrum and vital for extending a love of literature and the humanities into the future.

Second lesson: choose your battles. Social media can be devouring, a sinkhole for energy and time. Andrew Sullivan famously burned out on the relentless demands and told the tale in "I Used to Be a Human Being" in the September 2016 issue of *New York Magazine*. "An endless bombardment of news and gossip and images has rendered us manic information addicts. It broke me. It might break you, too" (Sullivan). That is why it has to be used strategically, to build networks, audiences, and alliances. I know the power of *Instagram*, *Tumblr*, *Reddit*—though I haven't had the hours, focus, or energy to pursue them. I've ignored Snapchat and Tiktok—perhaps I simply don't see their nontrivial potential. Each one is a whole new game with a whole new set of new rules. Each is a language and a city—a virtual state with its own laws and its own customs.

It is still astonishing to me how few otherwise savvy communicators—and academics—use social media to their advantage and how many resist learning how to achieve results with it. However, when there is a sense of mission, everyone can find a way to get involved with technology. The importance of networking cannot be overstated: it put me in touch with so many people who were vital to my work and my life—and it kept me in touch with them through the years.

Allow me to describe a few of the experiments I made to create a bigger public audience for books, literature, and human thought at Stanford and in the world beyond, and all were supported by my social media efforts. The first, my high-traffic blog *The Book Haven*, is a solo effort, which initially met with some resistance from Stanford bureaucracy. The second, a public "book club" called Another Look, is a team effort. And in the third, the radio/podcast series *Entitled Opinions*, I am entirely in service to someone else's legacy.

The Oxbridge Experiment: The Book Haven

A provocative reflection from a stranger can change one's world, and *Vanity Fair* editor Graydon Carter's musings altered mine a decade ago. He was reminiscing about the journalistic facility of Christopher Hitchens. In particular, he remembered a lunch at a local French restaurant. "I may have played with a glass of wine to be convivial. Hitchens had five good-size glasses of red, followed by a couple of tumblers of scotch as a palate cleanser," he recalled. "I came back to the office on fumes; Hitchens was completely unaffected by the intake. We sat him down at a borrowed desk in front of an old electric typewriter and he banged out 1,500 words on some subject or other. And it was so beautifully written as to make you want to cry" (Prout).

Hitchens was not alone. One might reference a few other Brits: Anthony Lane, Andrew Sullivan, Tina Brown. What do they have in common? They were educated at Oxford or Cambridge, which have a long-standing tutorial system. In a 2001 article in *The New York Review of Magazines*, Katie Prout explained: "In the tutorial system, the professor assigns an examination-style question to the student, hands him or her a lengthy bibliography from which to work, and expects the student to return the next week, ready to discuss and vigorously defend the eight pages he or she has written on the subject, thus learning to think, write and debate. And this happens week after week," Prout wrote. The system of education guarantees that students are able to go into intellectual battle, with a tough one-on-one discussion of the subject at hand.

I was never a student at Oxford or Cambridge, but as I read, I wondered if there was a way, even at a mature stage of my career, I could reignite—not by defending a paper with an Oxford don but by writing so much I would "break the sound barrier," so to speak, producing more persuasive, cleaner, more incisive writing on a tighter turnaround. Winston Churchill did precisely that, keeping to a disciplined daily schedule of relentless productivity. After long, champagne-fueled dinners every night at his country house,

Chartwell, Churchill padded up to his study, where he dictated his speeches and books to a team of waiting secretaries until about 4 a.m. He lived by his pen, and his output was astonishing; it earned him a Nobel Prize for Literature in 1953. At this time in my life also, the Stanford News Service was demanding that we produce more copy, faster. Might this do the trick, without Churchill's Chartwell stenographers?

None of us could produce the academically sound reportage on the near-daily basis that was demanded, but I'm told I came closest—an honor, especially since a former Associated Press reporter was on our News Service team, and that tribe is trained for hourly deadlines and daunting turn-around times. To accomplish my mission, I created a blog on the Stanford Web site. *The Book Haven* gave me an engine and a platform I never anticipated in my craziest dreams.

My intention was to create a forum for short items of news, that could be produced quickly, carried by the "voice" of the blogger (myself), and, as it would be informally written, bypassing the time-consuming formalities that even standard "news briefs" require. Its mandate would be wide: "a blog for the written word," as I called it, could include coverage of books, media articles, essays, or even other blogs. It would even give me the flexibility to venture occasionally into films or art. The News Service was suspicious: How often would I publish? How long would the pieces be? Who would read them? What if I ran out of material? Few, even in 2009, were aware of the great blogosphere and the versatility, freedom, and power it offered. At a time when the News Service was moving to hierarchical conformity rather than staff-generated innovation, this initiative bucked the trend. Management was wary about giving me the independence and power of a public voice. I was told to start a "practice" blog on a free Wordpress site, which I did. A few weeks after I had moved onto the Stanford Web site, the assistant vice president for communications called me in to tell me the site would be pulled unless I got my numbers up. (Nota bene: no one has good numbers in the first few weeks—readers must be earned, and it takes time to build traffic.)

The Book Haven would eventually be discussed in *The Guardian* and *The Atlantic*. Andrew Sullivan, one of my Oxbridge role models for productivity, featured the *The Book Haven* in *The Atlantic Wire*, *The Daily Beast*, and his own blog *Dish*—particularly when my stand against singer Cat Steven's unrepented support for Salman Rushdie's fatwa received widespread coverage. *The Book Haven* was linked by *The New Yorker* and named a top blog by

College Education Online. Eventually, it rose to forty-five thousand-page views per month. But all that was in the future. I started out as everyone else does, with a handful of page views per week.

The network I created supported me in offline ventures, too—when I later published a book, for example. Bloggers are usually journalists, reviewers, and authors, after all. Via *The Book Haven*, I "met" leading academics, journalists, cultural figures, and others—for instance, historian Timothy Snyder, who wrote a guest post to discuss his newly published *Bloodlands*. I connected with literary scholars and cultural journalists internationally.

I was receiving invitations to speak all over the world for my books, and wherever I went, people would know *The Book Haven*. I was offered (and took) two all-expense-paid trips to Poland through the connections I made. More recently, I attracted the attention of John Milton's Cottage, which resulted in my inaugural residency at the poet's only surviving residence in Chalfont St. Giles, Buckinghamshire. This year also, *The Book Haven* led to an invitation for an all-expense-paid trip to be a guest at the inaugural Bergen Literary Festival in Norway to interview the Croatian writer and Neustadt award-winner Dubravka Ugrešić for *Music & Literature*.

Let me chronologically list a few memorable high points of a decade of blogging:

When I was tipped off in late 2010 that a new edition of Mark Twain's *Huckleberry Finn* was excising the N-word, my blogpost about its publication went around the world, getting a big spread in *The New York Times*, and coverage in *The Guardian*, the BBC, and some of the continental media as well. *The Chronicle of Higher Education* credited *The Book Haven* with starting the worldwide conversation.

When *The Washington Post* invited readers to make funny captions for a photo of the aging, frizzy-haired Donald Hall as he received a National Medal of Arts from President Obama in 2011, I responded with a post that eminent, elderly poets (in this case, an octogenarian cancer survivor, too) should not be targeted for such ridicule. Others joined in, including, oddly enough, Sarah Palin in a tweet. *The Chronicle of Higher Education* took up the defense.

I was dismayed that even critics who reviewed the 2012 film *Les Misérables* claimed the action of Victor Hugo's classic took place during the French Revolution. They should have known better. Hence my blogpost "Enjoy *Les Misérables*. But Please Get the History Straight." The post got one hundred and fifty responses—a record—before I turned the comments off.

It also made me a guest speaker and informal consultant when *Les Mis* came to Stanford. The post is still viewed so often that I suspect it is finding a new life in classrooms.

Author Philip Roth announced he had retired from writing and giving media interviews—until Stanford's Another Look book club featured his *The Ghost Writer* in 2014. I asked him for an interview, and I got one. *The Book Haven* Q&A caught fire and was picked up around the world, leading to an article about Roth and *The Book Haven* in the pages of *The Guardian* and *The Los Angeles Times*. The interview was republished in translation in *Le Monde*, *La Repubblica*, and *Die Welt*. (It wasn't *The Book Haven*'s first time in *Le Monde*, however. When I wrote about Anaïs Saint-Jude's research on the communications revolution of the seventeenth century—which bore more than a passing resemblance to our own times—the French daily spotlighted the piece on page 1, and the post even got a mention in *The New Yorker*.)

In 2017, I broke the news nationally that President Trump intended to eliminate both the National Endowment for the Arts (NEA) and the National Endowment for the Humanities (NEH)—thanks to another tip. I could only claim an "exclusive" for a few hours, however, before the nation was on the story. I urged a letter-writing campaign. But I also explained that the agencies could not be eliminated by a president, and that both the NEA and NEH had bipartisan congressional support. For that prognostication, which turned out to be true, I was flamed and even "unfriended" by a prominent editor of my acquaintance, whose emotions outpaced his sanity. I was vindicated when not only did both agencies survive but they received an uptick in funding.

The Book Haven celebrates its tenth anniversary in 2019—no doubt a cake and champagne would be appropriate, but I doubt I'll have time to do much more than make a self-commemoratory blogpost, if I remember to do so. Would I recommend starting a blog today? It depends. I got in at the right time, and the flexibility and ingenuity I learned are transferrable skills for me, whatever the future brings. But could it be done today? I'm not sure.

The market has become saturated, and blogs have been displaced by platforms such as *Medium*, *Tumblr*, and even *Facebook*—"microblogging" has brought me traffic, but it is a world of its own and one that would take a good deal of time to master. The Internet landscape has changed in other ways. Landmarks are disappearing: This year, the literary blog *The Millions* was acquired by *Publishers Weekly* for an undisclosed price, and although *PW* says nothing will change, something already has. *Bookslut* shut its doors in 2016. In *The Guardian*, the blog's creator, Jessa Crispin, reminisced about the early days when she created the literary blog and webzine: "Back then, the online book culture was run mostly by enthusiasts and amateurs, people who were creating blogs and webzines simply for the pleasure of it, rather than to build a career or brand.... I regret the day money found the internet. Once advertisers showed up, offering to pay us to do the thing we were doing just for fun, it was very hard to say no. Or understand exactly what the trade-offs would be," she wrote. "Your revenue stream is linked directly to how many clicks and page views you stack up, and that eight-thousand-word interview with a Nigerian author published in English for the first time just isn't going to draw the crowds" (Crispin).

For me, *The Book Haven* has been, and continues to be, an adventure, and one that has opened me up to a worldwide network of writers, authors, and journalists. I'm told that the blog as a platform continues to work for those who monetize, and the reasons for getting onboard are commercial—however, dollars aren't a motivation on a university Web site, and fortunately, although I have used *The Book Haven* for a wide range of practical purposes, I do not survive by clicks. No one is counting them except me. Nor have I any wish to go independent. When I get a spam attack (on one crazy day, spam posts were pouring in five times faster, minute by minute, than I could furiously delete them), or when my Web site crashes, I'm grateful for the Stanford tech desk. "Going pro" would mean being a master of my own ship but also with maintenance and technological responsibilities I don't have the time or skills to take on.

When *The Book Haven* began, I was not the author of a celebrated book that went into multiple printings in its first year, and I now have three more books forthcoming in the next year. The commitment of authorial time and energy means I will, at the very least, be posting less often yet always mindful that blogging is a way to promote my books. Is it over? Blogging is often a place to try out new ideas and keep up with the world outside my own brain. It's an experience I wouldn't change for the world, and I'm not ready to bow out yet.

And while a prophet is usually not recognized in his country, I eventually got recognition even at Stanford. *The Book Haven* is being preserved by the university archives, to be part of the university's permanent record.

The Best Fiction You've Never Read: The Another Look Book Club

In 2012, the distinguished author Tobias Wolff, a recipient of the National Medal of the Arts, approached me with an idea: he wanted to create a forum where Stanford writers, scholars, and also literary figures from the world beyond Stanford could talk books with the San Francisco Bay Area community. The seasonal public event series, to be held three times a year, would spotlight connoisseurs' choices for books you must read—discussed and even championed by the people who love them. He wanted the first offering to be a cherished favorite, William Maxwell's *So Long, See You Tomorrow*. He asked me if I could make it all happen. I have to say I was doubtful. Book clubs did not have good associations for me. But as we talked more, I realized my reservations were twofold: first, I figured most people, like me, didn't have the time, especially hours and hours, to read hefty tomes of other people's choosing; and second, the chosen books tended to be mainstream, middlebrow, middle-of-the-road "safe" choices.

Inspired by Maxwell's novel, we decided that we would focus on short books—short enough for Bay Area professionals who are pressed for time and who may spend their days reviewing legal briefs, medical documents, or technical manuals. They might be enthusiastic for an ingenuous off-the-beaten-track book if it could be read in one or two sittings. Also, we would focus on top-notch books that were forgotten, overlooked, or simply hadn't received the audience they merit. We would call it Another Look. We would find people who wanted to be part of the world of books and literature—a world that may have vanished once they left university. The format was easy: just show up. No membership fees, no meetings with minutes, no commitments.

We had a full house the first night, and our audiences have been steadily climbing since (so much so that we had to move to a larger venue). One high point among many: for Philip Roth's *The Ghost Writer*, we were joined by writers Michael Chabon and Ayelet Waldman. It was the only time to date we have featured the book of a living author. As already mentioned, my Q&A with Roth made the international press, and the high-profile Another Look was featured in *The Guardian*.

When Wolff announced his retirement in 2015, we announced that Another Look was going to close shop. Record numbers of people attended our last event for Albert Camus's *The Stranger* (a book, Wolff argued, that was more honored than read). One Stanford professor in the audience, the eminent author Robert Pogue Harrison, stepped forward that night to offer to assume the directorship of the program. The following February's event with Werner Herzog at Dinkelspiel Auditorium, discussing J. A. Baker's *The Peregrine*, was a remarkable change of pace. The video is now available on *YouTube*, in both full-length and highlights version (Herzog). The event was covered by *San Francisco Chronicle* columnist Caille Millner, and the video was picked up by the Web site *Open Culture*.

It's rewarding to be the point of contact with our book-loving community—not just in the Bay Area, but sometimes around the nation and world, as people from far-flung places tell me they're reading along with us. Wolff has extolled the program during his speaking engagements around the country. The audience for our *Another Look* podcast series is growing, and we'll soon be adding YouTube videos. We've developed a subscribers' list that is nearing two thousand members. I'm told the size of the proprietary mailing list, and the caliber of its subscribers, is an asset that's unique at Stanford.

Why am I so keen on this program? Because it's rocked my world. My days and weeks are spent writing about a handful of writers and thinkers who are passions. However, as a result, there are huge holes in my *general* knowledge of modern fiction, and particularly US fiction. Without too much investment of time, I've caught up with significant writers I'd somehow missed along the way.

And along the way we've made a difference: For authors whose classic works were truly neglected, the attention was welcomed by the authors' literary estates and publishers—the events for Anita Loos's comic classic *Gentlemen Prefer Blondes* and Walter Tevis's *The Queen's Gambit* come to mind. Several of the books have reemerged from obscurity and received the fresh attention we'd hoped for. For example, on the highly ranked *The Millions* book blog, Italo Calvino's 1965 *Cosmicomics* shot up to number five on *Amazon*'s stats-based "best seller" list. There was no other reason for the surge except that it was the seasonal pick for Another Look.

From Audio to Text: Entitled Opinions

The Book Haven is a solo triumph; Another Look is teamwork. But my work with *Entitled Opinions* is a humble service to someone else's legacy in the humanities—in this case, a Stanford faculty member, but it was an effort that nevertheless was born of my own initiative in 2017.

Robert Harrison's radio show *Entitled Opinions* has devoted fans all over the world—from Australia to China, Mexico to Russia. One blogger called the intellectually powered interviews, broadcast from KZSU (90.1 FM) and available for free download on iTunes, "[O]ne of the most fascinating, engaging podcasts in any possible universe." (Harrison is also an acclaimed author and regular contributor to *The New York Review of Books*.) He has recorded about two hundred and thirty conversations since 2005, featuring some of our era's leading figures in literature, philosophy, science, and cultural history, including Richard Rorty, René Girard, Peter Sloterdijk, Shirley Hazzard, Orhan Pamuk, Colm Tóibín, Marilynne Robinson, Paul Ehrlich, Michel Serres, Hayden White, and Abraham Verghese. Yet Harrison had never received a penny to support more than a decade of programming, and he learned on his own the technical side of radio broadcasting—first for a KZSU Stanford radio show and Web site and then offered free through *iTunes* as well.

For many around the world, *Entitled Opinions* is a lifeline to the bigger universe of intellectual thought. Perhaps most moving are the letters and emails received from those in places where they find the program a lifeline; one woman in Pakistan protested the intellectually stultifying effects of a brutal religious fundamentalism and emailed that, with *Entitled Opinions*, she was "finally getting my oxygen." Another listener emailed to say: "your show accompanied me through pretty stressful times of intense military and political conflicts in Israel, when heavy objects were falling from the sky on both sides of the border and people were saying pretty dreadful things about other people. . . . The shows certainly helped me remain sane" (Haven, "Robert Harrison's radio show.")

Clearly, *Entitled Opinions*, available on *iTunes*, was no secret. But I thought it should be better known, familiar to everyone who loves literature, philosophy, ideas. There were reasons it wasn't. In 2017, the *Entitled Opinions* Web site still used the antiquated HTML format, with a long, unmemorable, alphabet-soup URL. Searching for past shows was clumsy and often impossible. Visitors had to scroll down through a seemingly endless chronological list of past episodes to find what they were looking for. Its future seemed at the mercy of technological advances.

I teamed with Harrison to plan for a bigger future for *Entitled Opinions*. A generous donation from former Stanford president John Hennessy helped fund a Web site redesign, with easily searchable programming and a home of its own that was not in a hard-to-find corner of the French and Italian department Web site.

I argued that there was nothing on either the new or old Web site to indicate what a listener would hear in the particular podcast, a powerful disincentive for anyone thinking to invest an hour. Not everyone will gamble their precious minutes that way. Jazz scholar Ted Gioia, a master of social media, had counseled me that the missing component in our modern cyber edifice is this: while there is much transferring of text to visual images, tweets, audio, and so on, there is comparatively little transfer going in the opposite direction—that is, turning audio and visual content into text. A few synoptic paragraphs with quotations from the episode would entice as well as inform potential listeners.

Entitled Opinions forged a partnership with *The Los Angeles Review of Books*, establishing a podcast channel for the program that would bring more visibility and draw new audiences. We also struggled to get a presence on social media—no small thing either, as Harrison was at first resistant to *Facebook*, *Twitter*, and the rest. He cherished the cult status of *Entitled Opinions* and emphasized the whole message of *Entitled Opinions* was for long thoughts over short ones, through the medium of intensive hour-long conversations. I was sympathetic. But in today's world, to get the word out without using social media is to try to get the word out without getting the word out.

Now we are taking the next step: we are creating lightly edited transcripts and pitching them to international media to spread the word about *Entitled Opinions*. Harrison's interview with German philosopher Peter Sloterdijk ran in translation in *Die Welt*. The original English transcript is forthcoming in *The Los Angeles Review of Books*. The first of a two-part interview with French thinker René Girard ran in England's *Standpoint*; the second is scheduled for Zurich's *Neue Zürcher Zeitung*, which has also run a translation of Harrison's interview with US philosopher Richard Rorty. More are on the way.

How long will we hold back time? The MP3 format is already a little passé, and I don't know who will be around in the coming decades to transfer two or three hundred recorded interviews, some of them of historic importance, to the next media format. Far-fetched? It's happening already in other media. Bits of our culture are disappearing, without fanfare or protest. For example, the renowned film *A Month in the Country*—Another

Look featured J. L. Carr's 1980 masterpiece in 2015—may no longer exist in a high-quality original. It's happened more locally with Stanford News Service videos that are lost or irretrievable. People trust the cloud to save us, but there's nothing as impermanent as a cloud.

This project, more than the others, made me aware of our how much the transient is in service to the enduring. It's part and parcel with public scholarship in the modern era. So many of these castles in the air will go poof, and as I write this retrospective of my work with literary public scholarship, I have retraced my steps and discovered so many broken links, so many Web sites that have disappeared, so much that has vanished behind a paywall or is otherwise irretrievable. It's the nature of our evanescent cyber sphere, our provisional time. That's why, in the end, I'm mistrustful of anything that doesn't have a print component—hence, my recent effort with *Entitled Opinions*.

The closest thing that our government has to eternity is the Library of Congress. I know paper can burn in a flash fire, get swept away in a flood, or eaten by locusts, but I think it's still the best "technology" we've got. But then, I started out in newspapers.

—January 2019, Palo Alto

Works Cited

"'The Book Haven': A New Blog for Stanford's Literary Universe." *Stanford Report*, 2 Feb. 2010, https://news.stanford.edu/news/2010/february1/book-haven-release020210.html.

Crispin, Jessa. "Bookslut Was Born in an Era of Internet Freedom: Today's Web Has Killed It." *The Guardian*, 16 May 2016.

Harrison, Robert Pogue. "A Messenger of the Rope: In Conversation with Peter Sloterdijk." *Los Angeles Review of Books*, 10 July 2019.

———. "Die Demokratie hat mehr zum Glück beigetragen als Buddha." *Neue Zürcher Zeitung*, 16 Feb. 2019, pp. 44–45.

———. "Shakespeare: Mimesis and Desire: A Dialogue between René Girard and Robert Pogue Harrison." *Standpoint*, Dec. 2018/Jan. 2019, no. 107, pp. 56–63.

———. "René Girard: 'Wir reden so viel über Sex, weil wir es nicht wagen, über Neid zu sprechen.'" *Neue Zürcher Zeitung*, 4 Aug. 2019.

Haven, Cynthia L. "Robert Harrison's Radio Show, 'Entitled Opinions,' Gets a New Look." *Stanford Report*, 17 Oct. 2017, https://news.stanford.edu/thedish/2017/10/17/robert-harrisons-radio-show-entitled-opinions-gets-a-new-look/.

———. "'Only Silence Is Innocent': Zagajewski on Rilke, Irony, and the Future of

Poetry." *The Book Haven*, 21 June 2011, http://bookhaven.stanford.edu/2011/06/only-silence-is-innocent-adam-zagajewski-on-rilke/.

———, editor. *Conversations with René Girard: Prophet of Envy*. Bloomsbury, 2020.

Herzog, Werner. "Legendary Werner Herzog Talks about Books with author Robert Pogue Harrison." *YouTube*, posted by Stanford, 16 Feb. 2016, https://www.youtube.com/watch?v=n4b7vBWwbuo&t=343s.

Prout, Katie. "The Britishisation of American Magazines." *New York Review of Magazines*, 2001, http://archives.jrn.columbia.edu/nyrm/2001/features/brits.html.

Ray, Elaine. "So Many Books, So Little Coverage." *Stanford Report*, 15 Dec. 2009, https://news.stanford.edu/thedish/2009/12/15/so-many-books-so-little-coverage/.

Sullivan, Andrew. "I Used To Be a Human Being." *New York Magazine*, vol. 19, Sep. 2016, http://nymag.com/intelligencer/2016/09/andrew-sullivan-my-distraction-sickness-and-yours.html.

Takin' It to the Streets

Public Scholarship in the Heartland

Carmaletta M. Williams

> Certain things are clear. First, the corpus of Black American literature is predicated upon culturally specific values and experiences. Second, the literature must be viewed in a historical spectrum since it serves as a cultural mirror.
> —Houston A. Baker Jr.,
> "On the Criticism of Black American Literature"

As amazing and gratifying as the experience proved to be, spending my professional career as a professor of English and African American studies at a community college in Kansas came with its own peculiar set of issues. About two years into my career, Elizabeth, a dear, smart, young white student, came to me as the class was ending. With a warm smile on her face, an A paper in her hand, and positive atmosphere around her, she ever so sweetly told me that she was glad she had taken my class. Not only had she been learning so much information that she had never been exposed to before, but I was the first "colored" teacher she had ever had. Both of these new experiences, she confessed, were amazing catalysts to expanding her world.

This young woman obviously meant well. She was, after all, giving me two compliments at once. Referring to me by a precivil-rights-enlightenment era label certainly wasn't meant to be an insult. But I was insulted. Taken aback to being referred to as *colored*, a term that hadn't really been used to refer to African Americans for over fifty years, long before she was born, I fought hard to keep the smile on my face and quietly exhale. Sure, the word *colored* as a reference to African Americans is a seldom used but active adjective, not a noun. Like *Negro*, it had long passed into racial archives. This incident with Elizabeth happened two decades before former acting chair of the Democratic National Committee, Donna Brazile, penned her book *For Colored Girls Who Have Considered Politics* (2018), riffing the title off Ntozake Shange's landmark choreopoem *For Colored Girls Who Have Considered Suicide / When the Rainbow Is Enuf* (1976), which was written forty years earlier than Brazile's tome. Immediately, I knew the source of my angst. I had read Maya Angelou's autobiography *I Know Why the Caged Bird Sings*. Like Angelou, I had determined at a very young age that no white child would ever call me by my first name, unless they were my personal friends. When many of my colleagues were saying that it was alright for their students to call them by their first names, I stood adamantly opposed. Students always asked, "What should we call you?" Which in itself struck me as an odd question. But I'm old school, and there was never any ambivalence. The teacher was "Mr." or "Ms." and whatever their last name happened to be. But I held back, and my response was always given with a smile, "You may call me, Dr. Williams, Professor Williams, or even [with a deep gulp] Ms. Williams." That also came from Dr. Angelou. Calling me by any other name would be the ultimate disrespect. Even though Elizabeth had not called me Carma, as the poor white girl with dirty panties had called Angelou's grandmother, by her given name, I had no doubt that my reaction had nothing to do with Elizabeth as a person but was rooted in having a young white girl call me *colored*. That just would not have happened with an African American student. This was about racial recognition and respect for my race.

As I wondered where in the world had she been that she didn't know that African Americans were not called "colored" anymore, other students were still mingling in the room and one "enlightened" young white man (there was only one student of color in the class and she had absolutely no interest in getting involved in the discussion) loudly pronounced with a superior tone in his voice, "Colored? You called her 'colored!' *We* can't call *them* colored anymore." Uncomfortable laughter from the other students rippled caustically through the room. I certainly felt my "hackles" rising. More insulted by his dichotomous division of *my* classroom, I called a halt to the discussion. "Let's think about the way we label people, the historical imperatives involved in the naming, and for what reasons," I instructed in my sternest professorial voice more to quiet Craig than anything else. "Next class period that's what our discussion will be." As the students groaned and filed out of the room with complaints of "see what you did? More work. I already have too much to do. What's historical imperative?" I knew I had the answer to my own question of "Where had she been?" Obviously, in a racial bubble somewhere. Elizabeth might have come from one of the remote rural areas of Kansas where people of color were rare. Or, from some of the smaller towns where communities self-identified by their ethnic origins or chosen professions. Or, maybe even from Johnson County, the site of the college, where the mostly transplanted population sees itself as positive, productive, upwardly mobile, and white, an identification to which they were determined to cling. As witness of this, in my nearly thirty years at the college, no other African Americans had been hired for full-time positions in the humanities.

So, what was next? I certainly could expand upon the teachable moment Elizabeth had created in my classroom, but that would do little about getting to the source of the problem. I needed to reach those people who apparently comfortably used archaic racial terms in their day-to-day lives. I was going to hit the streets to share knowledge with the uninformed about African American people. They would understand why dear, sweet Elizabeth insulted me with her kind words. That lesson could truly only be taught by someone whose reality was inherent in the maligned culture. I wrapped my African American Super Woman cloak around my shoulders and committed myself to expanded teaching, which now included public scholarship.

Imagining America defines public scholarship as "scholarly or creative activity that joins serious intellectual endeavor with a commitment to public practice and public consequence" (Carleton College, "What Is Public Scholarship?"). It was the last part that caused hesitancy. My commitment then became to make sure that my work was positive and that it evoked a productive, progressive response from the people with whom I was going to share my knowledge of African American life and culture. If, according to *Imagining America*, public scholarship meant that I would have to merge the scholarly and creative work that I used in my university teaching with my community partners, my launch into this new arena would be a walk in the park. I had been very successful in my educational career, both as a student and a professor, in a large part because I have always focused on making my work accessible to a reading public. I was also very comfortable in knowing that I had very good mastery of the material. I had learned it and lived it. Connecting with my students, who, for the most part, were all very bright and eager to learn, was prime training ground for my new mission. Bright as stars and eager as all get-out, those students were also college freshmen and sophomores, with a knowledge base comparable to many of the people I would encounter in the communities I would visit. I never, ever "dumbed" down my classroom lectures. It was important to me that students leaving my classroom knew the context and language of our subject and had or acquired scholarly language and vocabulary during our tenure together. What I would have to do for my public classrooms is create lesson plans around the book or theme that we would be addressing, then present the information in a "non-teacherly" way. I would not lecture. I would not question their understanding of the material, and I certainly would not assign homework. Instead, I would draw them into the lesson by providing background materials in an entertaining way that would make them feel safe to discuss race.

It would be nearly thirty years before I'd be awarded an Emmy for my portrayal of Harlem Renaissance novelist, folklorist, autobiographer Zora Neale Hurston, but in libraries, community centers, and theaters around the world, I rehearsed the artistic, critical, and historical work that contributes to public debates. Crosby Kemper III, then director of the Kansas City Public Library in partnership with Kansas City Public Television, produced and starred in *Meet the Past*, a program in which Kemper interviewed historical characters. My dear friend the late Henry Fortunato called me one day and asked if I would perform as Hurston with Crosby on the program. I am always eager to share Hurston with others, so I agreed. I had never met Kemper, so we scheduled a production meeting. Late, as I understand is customary for him in those situations, Kemper entered the elegant boardroom with stacks of books on and by Hurston. After a brief hello, he very seriously looked at me and announced that those were the books I would have to read to be successful in this program. I looked at Fortunato who was beyond blood red trying to stifle his laughter. I turned to Kemper and said, "Are any of my works in there?" Fortunato could hold it no longer. I said, "Henry, you didn't vet me to him?" His response was, "No. I wanted to see the look on his face when he realized who he was meeting with." Kemper saw nothing funny. The night of the performance, the room was packed with people of all races, ages, and purposes for the filming of the show. It was gratifying but hard to stay in character, as so many of my relatives, friends, and associates had heard of my work and had come to hear Hurston's story. The questions were excellent and addressed diverse aspects of the presentation from the Harlem Renaissance, Hurston's personal past and her works, and how the Works Progress Administration (WPA) work was beneficial for capturing African American life and history. I have dubbed the Emmy Crosby's and my beautiful love child, as giving birth to her was truly laborious but rewarding.

I accepted public scholarship as being at the center of the Venn diagram of reciprocity, civic responsibility, creativity, and public knowledge as developed by Carleton College ("What Is Public Scholarship?"). In order to help wonderful students like Elizabeth and the people in her communities, I would have to take my scholarship to the streets of the Heartland. Rosemary Erickson Johnsen, in her work "Public Scholarship: Making the Case," cites the definition by *Imagining America* of public scholarship, which serves as a guide for this work: "Scholarly or creative activity that encompasses different forms of making knowledge about, for, and with diverse publics and communities" (Johnsen 10). Like educator Marie Troppe, who acknowledges that most of her work has been a "hybrid . . . translation between expert models of knowledge . . . and experience models of knowledge, which are often embodied in community-based organizations or networks" ("From 19th Century"), I grasped that in order to reach those diverse communities, my teaching would have to reach beyond the smart boards, whiteboards, and even my favorite chalkboards to be a blend of styles, forums, and approaches. This was going to be fun. I deeply agree with David Domke who argues that "we have a duty, a social responsibility, to offer these perspectives in lay terms for those who are interested . . . It is not acceptable for me to write for and teach only the few who attend my university or read the academic journals I publish in. I owe the public more" (qtd. in Johnsen 15). Public scholarship arises, in part, then, from an ethical call to engage with the public intellectually, to be citizen scholars. Second, public scholarship rewards us as individual scholars. The exchange of ideas with people who are neither our colleagues nor family is enriching.

The Kansas Humanities Council (KHC, now Humanities Kansas) provided the initial out-of-the-classroom forums I needed to reach my conquests, and I, armed with my repertoire of teaching styles, was ready to launch my public scholarship activities. I had to educate Elizabeth's folks, her teachers, and all the people who lived around them. I was David out to slay Goliath, the "Uninformed Racial Giant." It was the early '90s, I was in my thirties, and more than eager to right some racial wrongs. Being the only Black professor in the humanities department in a predominantly white institution had instilled a frustration that surfaced with Elizabeth's comment. I was the Sistah with the big Afro, fist in the air and militant attitude. I had witnessed the Civil Rights Movement from my living-room television because my mother refused to let me march anywhere, except to my bedroom if I said another word about it, so now was my time to make a difference in race relations.

Almost immediately after signing up for the KHC Speaker's Bureau and Talk About Literature in Kansas (TALK) programs, I started receiving many invitations to speak at libraries and community centers across the state. I wondered what the attraction to me was. I didn't look like, speak like, or have any of the same social or political ideologies of the people who were asking me to come into their towns. Maybe it was my difference that was magnetizing. Did they really want to learn about African American literature and culture, or was I going to be some kind of sideshow, a novelty to them? A means for them to assuage some liberal guilt. They could say they tried, even had a Black woman in to explain "it" to them, but they still don't get it. Well, there was no way on God's green earth that I was going to let that happen. Well versed with the books and lectures I was to give, my only hesitancy was what to expect in the interactions with my audiences. I adopted the Zora Neale Hurston stance that if they didn't like me, it was their loss—I am an amazing person—but I also knew that all lands outside of urban centers were foreign to me. I just am not a country girl, but I determined to not ever think "bumpkin" when I went into their communities. The lessons I needed to teach had to be given in all sorts of venues, and I had to take the anthropological stance and gauge them all on their particular merits—not compare them to my reality. But like Langston Hughes, in his autobiography *I Wonder as I Wander*, there was a nagging question: "Would they like me?" Having been brought up with brothers who refused to let me be cowardly toward anything, I took a deep breath, gathered up my books and talking points, and hit the streets.

My mission, then, became not just to educate the students in my classes but also to take those lessons down the highways and byways of the state to educate those persons who were teaching those young people like Elizabeth. I was going to ease on down Kansas roads carrying to the people my knowledge of African American life and culture. And even if they didn't like it, they would have to respect me and my heritage. Maybe it wouldn't be hard. David Hume, after all, asserts that the taste of an intelligent person is enough to judge a literary work. Since I was carrying with me aspects of art, especially African American literature, which Houston A. Baker Jr. defines as "that body of written works crafted by authors consciously (even, at times, self-consciously) aware of the long-standing values and significant experiences of their culture" (113), and I knew that literature well, I felt I was armed for whatever battle was ahead. I fully anticipated those crowds at the public places where I would be teaching to be rooted in their own historical imperatives. I expected there to be two possibilities: either I would be preaching to a crowd that was fully open to accepting the expressions and revelations of difference as inherent in African American art on an equal basis to their cadre of "important" writers, or it would be people so rigid in their feelings that in order to be "important," African American art would have to be integrative—meaning, of course, that it would have to mirror white American art. Either way, interpreting African American art, for people who had no insight into the culture, would not be an easy task, but it was one I was joyfully anticipating.

William J. Harris identifies Black poet and playwright Amiri Baraka as "the main artist-intellectual responsible for shifting the emphasis of contemporary black literature from an integrationist art conveying a raceless and classless vision to a literature rooted in the black experience" (Hill 1370). As I grabbed my bag containing a notebook, in case I heard something profound I could immediately write it down and not lose it "bird by bird," as Anne Lamott warns, and a copy of Zora Neale Hurston's *Their Eyes were Watching God*, my Black literary mainstay, I strolled into the library in south central Kansas. On my way in, I acknowledged that although I've had a fair amount of success in publications of my research and other writing, I am a far lesser artist-intellectual than Baraka and wondered how I could help *these people* understand the African American experience in literature. What would they be expecting? What had they thought of the book? What was their criteria for labeling works by African Americans as "art"? Would they paint with broad strokes as typical of all Black people Hurston's use of vernacular language? Would they think of it as "broken English" and not recognize it as a complete language system? Would they look down on the Black American experience because of the dialectical language? Surely, they must. Why wouldn't they? Many African Americans whose personal experiences and racial history are captured in these books have the same view, and this, after all, was Kansas, where the people are stuck in a deep evolutionary abyss between civilization in the urban centers on the eastern side of the state and the wide mountain openness of Colorado on the west.

As I strolled into their communities, it didn't take long for me to learn that I'm the one who had to make some massive shifts in understanding racial realities. The patrons at most of the events were white. Occasionally an African American woman and her husband, who would smile and had read the book but looked as if he was only there to make his wife happy, would be present but Black people at these sessions were rare. All of the people were friendly, shook my hand, patted me on my back, and walked me to the table with the treats and coffee they had brought. They did all they could to make me feel welcome. Saying "people are people everywhere" is trite and largely untrue, but what I came to realize is that the folks who came out to the libraries and community centers were thinking people and very cognizant that racial differences are real and ultimately reflected in the literature. I applaud these people for their courage to ask direct questions and their willingness to have racial issues illuminated. I think they especially wanted the interpretations to come from a Person of Color.

At almost every session, someone asked if I would read a particular passage from whatever book we were discussing to them. I gladly agreed for two reasons: it filled the time that otherwise I would have used in explaining the writer's intentions, history, or something else that I would have hoped the readers could have seen on their own; and I like to perform. My one broad lesson at every session, wherever I was facilitating the discussions and regardless to composition of the audience, was to read aloud a passage from the book to demonstrate that vernacular English is very understandable. It is phonetic. It sounds exactly as it is written and the words are easily understood when heard. As I read and they followed along, I saw heads nodding and light bulbs flashing as suddenly the book made sense to them. My light bulb flashed as I understood that we only had to make small steps to cross those bridges to understanding.

I take those lessons with me to this day. Two years after I began my soirees into Kansas territory, I was invited to be a visiting scholar at a summer institute for high school teachers hosted by the Kansas Humanities Council. My role, along with three other scholars, was to work with those teachers on easy methods of incorporating ethnic literatures into their curriculum. Piece of cake. I had an arm full of turnkey lesson plans and a big smile. Halfway through the first morning, one teacher raised her hand, which was not required, to lament that she just didn't think she could do it. African American life and culture was so far removed from her life experiences that she just couldn't connect. Almost in lockstep, the other scholars and participants nodded their heads affirmatively. They all understood what she meant. I was dismayed. Really? Had she actually said such a thing out loud and meant it? Did these folks really empathize with her? I couldn't let her get away with such an asinine excuse for not teaching African American literature. Her commitment to not trying and her nonsensical logic struck me hard. I bet she was one of Elizabeth's teachers or related to one. In retrospect, I think I overreacted and still regret my response to her to a degree. But when she said that she just couldn't teach *Their Eyes Were Watching God* because it was too far out of her personal experience. I felt like I had been sucker punched and found myself jumping on her quickly. I just knew that it was time to stop the foolishness. Not to be a bully, but my work as an educator was now fully invested in making sure that unfounded assertions like hers did not make their way into curricula or even human thoughts. I had to confront this restricting ideation and save young people like Elizabeth. So, I stepped up. I brusquely asked if she had ever ridden a raft down the Mississippi. Of course, she hadn't, but she still taught Mark Twain. I asked her if she had ever stirred steaming cauldrons in the forest. Same answer. But she still taught Shakespeare. She had never lived in Haworth or London but adored the Brontë sisters. I may have even been shaking my finger at her by this time as I lectured to her on choice. She chose what she wanted to teach and left the rest. It was just a terrible loss for her students that she chose not to teach African American literature. That only happened once. Maybe the word spread or maybe, and hopefully, she was just an anomaly. My point had been made. But more than just correcting misguided ideas, I recognized that no longer would or could my teaching be confined to sharing knowledge with students in the classroom. My work now was permanently broader than the walls of academia. It now officially included public scholarship.

My job, I recognized, was to make the people at each and every session I facilitated feel as W. E. B. Du Bois, the foremost Black intellectual, in his essay "Criteria of Negro Art" (first published in *The Crisis* in 1926) describes as those nonacademics who feel relief at being able to discuss difficult topics such as social justice and fighting their fear of being uncomfortable in our session, to afterward have a new ability to "sit and dream of something which leaves a nice taste in the mouth" (17). My job then as a public scholar was not to beat them up for not knowing the subliminal messages in the works, or for not being aware of the historical implications in race relations, but to open their minds, accept newfound knowledge, and apply that to their continued learning. Our goal, after all, as Du Bois describes it, is to have our patrons know that African Americans, just like others, regardless of race or origin, desire "to be Americans, full-fledged Americans, with all the rights of other citizens" (17). Maybe, as Du Bois recognized during the early twentieth century, the thick little lady with her crochet needles and skeins of yarn in my workshop a century later, who had read and remembered every part of the book, had flashes of "clairvoyance, some clear idea, of what America really is" (17). She never missed a stitch when she told us that, as a child, she worked as a waitress at a roadside café in western Kansas. When the soldiers who were transporting POWs across the state to prison camps stopped at the café, the white soldiers and the prisoners were allowed to take tables in the front of the restaurant. The "colored" soldiers had to eat in a room in the back. "I made sure," she lifted her head in pride as she spoke, "that they got the best service possible. I couldn't do anything about them having to eat in the back, but I could make sure they got good food and good service." Her statement placed me smack in the middle of reciprocity, the top of the Venn diagram mentioned previously. She had become the teacher and I was the rigid, narrow-minded student. In public scholarship, the knowledge doesn't go just one way. Scholars learn from nonspecialists just as, hopefully, they learn from us. Other than the "colored" comment, that woman was probably one that taught Elizabeth to be kind and smart. She certainly taught and humbled me.

I agree with Du Bois that *we who are dark* have a special vision of the United States that is not shared with those who are not. I love being Black. I love that others can look at me and without a word being said know that I am proud of who I am. I knew from the first step on my public scholarship road that many of those participants would see me as representing *all* African Americans. This was repeatedly witnessed with statements of "you" and "you people." That second-person pronoun placed me smack in the center of the arena and made me responsible for and representative of anyone at any time who had ever had a drop of Black blood or spent a second immersed in a diverse culture. "You" referred to everyone possessing any portion of my race. That is amusing as well as confining. Amiri Baraka (LeRoi Jones) in his play *The Slave* (1964) is truly on point when he says: "But listen now . . . Brown is not brown except when used as an intimate description of personal phenomenological fields. As your brown is not my brown, et cetera, that is, we need, ahem, a meta-language. We need something not included here" (45). I certainly didn't have the missing "something," that language used to talk about language. I have my experiences as an African American woman, as a woman born and raised in these United States, and as a well-educated person. I deeply resent that my position as a well-educated person has shortcomings because there is much African American literature I will never be privileged to read because people in power who published books deemed stories of the Black experience not to be of the same value as those of whites. But that is comfortably embedded deep in my psyche. There is nothing I can do about that. Much of that art is lost, but recovery efforts of scholars such as Joycelyn K. Moody will bring the light of day to some of those writings. For me I knew then, as I know right now, that I couldn't carry that resentment into those community centers and libraries with me if I expected to be effective. That would not be good teaching. I would use the language I had, the one they understood.

I let the resentment of culture lost due to racism languish in the recesses of my mind. But, my mission became bigger than that. Like Du Bois, I knew that I had something special that I took into those streets and into those community facilities with me, the knowledge that "I am but an humble disciple of art.... I am one who tells the truth and exposes evil and seeks with Beauty and for Beauty to set the world right. That somehow, somewhere eternal and perfect Beauty sits above Truth and Right I can conceive, but here and now and in the world in which I work they are for me unseparated and inseparable" (Du Bois 19).

Taking the bifurcated language that is inherent in diverse cultures and blending them into a single voice that can be understood and experienced by all is an important aspect of public scholarship. I try hard in all my public teaching to make sure that I have not established adversarial positions. Participants in those community functions can then become informed critics of the Black aesthetic. Sharing the historical context of the art allows those readers to move from the broad, sweeping allusions and delusions of American America and the many other diverse people who live in these United States to a succinct realization that most historical texts were written to hide the realities inherent in the actions of those persons who attempted to eradicate the lives and art of diverse people. If you hide the beauty of a people, it is easier to feel superior to them. The ever-shifting majority may have established specificities and boundaries, defining the terms of what is art, but doing so certainly did little to advance an honest depiction of diverse cultures. Public scholars must provide the global and cultural contexts in which the work was created and include that information in every lecture, every performance, and every talk.

My platform has vastly expanded since those first steps on the public scholarship road. I have almost realized my goal of teaching on every continent except for the frozen ones. My goals and achievements have been comparable the world over. I want to bring methods of understanding of the lives, history, and culture of people of African descent, to folks everywhere. Ours is a story worth knowing. As a public scholar, I illuminate the historical effect of the pieces I present. When I perform as Harlem Renaissance novelist, folklorist, biographer, and anthropologist Zora Neale Hurston, she tells her audiences in Dodge City, Kansas; Paris, France; and Wuhan, Hubei Province in the People's Republic of China, *why* there is an Eatonville, Florida. In my Speaker's Bureau talk, "Free Did Not Mean Welcome" in establishing Kansas as a free state, I have to make the same painful point in Wichita, Kansas, as well as in Accra, Ghana, that "free state" status was enacted to keep Blacks of all stations, free or enslaved, out of the territory. Even fifty years after the emancipation of enslaved people, the teenage Carrie Hughes, who became mother of renowned poet and artist in many genres Langston Hughes, was the "Belle of *Black* Lawrence" because she could not have been the "Belle of Lawrence." (Williams and Tidwell). Making these explicit points moves the performance, reading, talk, etc. out of the realm of a "nice" visit to "scholarship"—public scholarship.

At the core of my self-determination to be a successful public scholar was my commitment to ensure that those people with whom I come in contact know that I am there as a teacher and scholar, to share my vision of beauty: a place and the space where we create art for ourselves and share it with our posterity, our communities, all of America, and the world. I cannot nor do I wish to go back to that day in my Composition II classroom when Elizabeth called me "colored" and launched taking my scholarship to the streets. Exchanging my education and experiences with people outside of my classroom has been amazingly rewarding. The interface between the realities of the people in my community college classes, my university classes around the world, my community workshops, my role now as executive director of the Black Archives of Mid-America, and my own personal reality has enriched my awareness of others and deepened my historical and cultural knowledge base. I no longer harbor any resentment toward the people who taught Elizabeth that *colored* was an appropriate term for African Americans. I am grateful for that catalyst into my public scholarship journey and the knowledge that what I have learned through formal education and have experienced as an African American woman in this country has to be shared beyond the red brick walls of an institution housing a classroom. I have to keep taking it to the streets.

Works Cited

Angelou, Maya. *I Know Why the Caged Bird Sings*. Random House, 1969.
Baker, Houston A, Jr. "On the Criticism of Black American Literature: One View of the Black Aesthetic." *African American Literature Theory: A Reader*, edited by Winston Napier, New York UP, 2000, pp. 113–31.
Baraka, Amiri [LeRoi Jones]. *Dutchman and The Slave: Two Plays by LeRoi Jones*. William Morrow and Company, 1964.
Brazile, Donna, Yolanda Caraway, Leah Daughtry, and Minyon Moore, with Veronica Chambers. *For Colored Girls Who Have Considered Politics*. Picador, 2019.
Carleton College. "What Is Public Scholarship?" *Center for Community and Civic Engagement*, https://www.carleton.edu/ccce/faculty/engaged-research-scholarship/what-is-public-scholarship/ Accessed 24 Oct. 2018.
Du Bois, W. E. B. *The Crisis*, vol. 32, Oct. 1926, pp. 290–97.
———. "Criteria of Negro Art." *African American Literary Theory: A Reader*, edited by Winston Napier, New York UP, 2000, pp. 17–23.
Hill, Patricia Liggins, editor. "Voices of the New Black Aesthetic." *Call and Response: The Riverside Anthology of the African American Literary Tradition*, Houghton Mifflin, 1998, p. 1370.
Hughes, Langston. *I Wonder as I Wander*. American Century Series, Hill & Wang, 1993.
Hurston, Zora Neale. *1937*. Harper Collins, 2013.
Johnsen, Rosemary Erickson. "Public Scholarship: Making the Case." *Modern Language Studies*, vol. 45, no. 1, 2015, pp. 8–19.
Troppe, Marie. "From 19th Century Benevolence Literature to 21st Century Activism." *Public*, vol. 2, no. 2, 2017, https://public.imaginingamerica.org/blog/article/hybrid-evolving-and-integrative-career-paths/.
Williams, Carmaletta, and John Edgar Tidwell, editors. *My Dear Boy: The Letters from Carrie Hughes to Langston Hughes 1926–1938*. U of Georgia P, 2013.

Linking Classrooms, Connecting Learning

The University of Washington Texts and Teachers Program

Gary Handwerk, Chris Chaney, and Anu Taranath

What do you get when you mix twelve to fifteen secondary-school teachers from eight high schools across four districts with three university faculty members, add lots of passion for close reading, cultural literacy, social justice, and critical pedagogy, and then let the ingredients marinate slowly and carefully for a decade or two? Welcome to the University of Washington's (UW) Texts and Teachers program, a unique high school/university collaborative partnership housed at the University of Washington's Seattle campus.

In the chapter that follows, we will provide a brief overview of the history of our now twenty-year-old partnership with regional Puget Sound high schools in offering dual-credit literature courses taken by high school students, all of which are regularly linked in ways that we describe below, with university courses at the University of Washington and Seattle Pacific University. Focusing on the program's infrastructure and ongoing operation, we want to offer suggestions to colleagues, administrators, and prospective teachers about what it takes to establish and to keep a program like ours alive. At the same time, we want to reflect more broadly about the nature and value of the kinds of literacy that humanities programs and courses typically seek to create.

What We Do: Program Basics

College professors and high school teachers codevelop and then simultaneously coteach a university course. The history and practices create a highly effective program.

For the last twenty years, the UW's Texts and Teachers program (UWTT) has been connecting university courses taught on our campus with equivalent courses in regional high schools across the Puget Sound area. This dual-credit program falls under the administrative umbrella of UW's Continuum College, which houses a number of similar programs in many different disciplines. Their UW in the High School (UWHS) program allows high school students to take university courses, taught by university-approved and university-trained high school teachers, in their high school classrooms—and potentially earn both high school credit and transferable college credit.[1] In the past five years, more than nineteen hundred high school students have enrolled in one of three Texts and Teachers courses, over half of them paying a reduced fee ($370 vs. $1,250 for five on-campus UW credits) to gain official college credit for their coursework. Over the same period, about seven hundred university students have taken these same classes on the campuses of UW and Seattle Pacific University (which partners with UW in sponsoring the program).

UWTT was born as an offshoot of a program developed at Brown University in the late 1980s, which ultimately received National Endowment of the Humanities (NEH) support to pursue possibilities for national expansion.[2] At various moments, a dozen New England universities and another half dozen across the country have been involved. As of 2018, the UW program is the only one still in existence—not just alive but thriving, with increasing numbers of teachers and students participating in the last several years. One goal of this chapter is to think through the implications of the apparent anomaly of this longevity in order to sharpen our understanding of what enables programmatic continuity. What does it take to create such programs, and to keep them alive? An even more central purpose for us, however, is to make a case for the value of *ongoing* university–high school collaborations and thus to suggest to colleagues in university and college settings that high school teachers and their students are among our most important public audiences and potential partners.

Two features make UWTT notably different from other university-sponsored humanities public-engagement activities. First, it is not a top-down program where we provide a curriculum and train teachers to use it but instead fully collaborative at every stage. It involves high school teachers from the start in helping design the courses that they will be teaching parallel to the university courses, making them partners in a shared educational project. Second, this program encourages in-person interaction between the college and high school classes. UWTT programs typically involve one visit by high school students to the university campus to participate in the linked course, along with one or more visits by the university faculty to each partner high school to do a day of classroom teaching there. The benefits of involvement flow in both directions, with teachers in the different settings sharing their educational experiences and expertise. All of us gain from this experience a much fuller awareness of the longer-term educational trajectory of these students; in a fundamental way, their students become ours, and ours become theirs.

Why We Do It: Teaching and Learning Outcomes

There are powerful multiplier effects that emerge from this fully collaborative and reciprocally respectful teaching-and-learning project.

Let's begin, though, with why. Why should higher education faculty members take on the, at best, modestly recompensed extra labor of connecting classes across different educational settings? Why should those of us teaching the humanities in higher education see high school students as one of *our* publics and, indeed, as one of the most important ones? At some level, the answer to these questions seems easy. As we all know, most teachers are more likely to do a better job of teaching when they work together. In addition, working across academic levels and systemic divides combats the pervasive curricular disarticulation that can create significant barriers to student success. But a foundational principle of UWTT is that we benefit the most by doing collaborative curricular work on the ground—school by school—and across time (i.e., that building and sustaining programmatic infrastructure and working relationships is crucial for long-term impact). We believe that possibilities for both curricular reform and professional development for teachers are strengthened when these two activities—all too often seen as separable[3]–are combined in the context of working together on a specific class, both at its inception and as it changes over time.

Curricular Transformation/Educational Articulation

That there are disconnects at almost every juncture across K–12 systems, community college systems, and four-year college/university systems is obvious to anyone who has been paying attention to US education. Nor is this a problem that seems to have lessened much in recent years; it is likely intrinsic to the decentralized nature of US educational systems (even in a world of Common Core requirements [Washington State Common Core Standards]).[4] From our perspective in the humanities, these disconnects can be seen as a matter of both content and skills. High school students do not always read the kinds or range of texts that we might prefer, and how they go about reading them can differ markedly from practices at the postsecondary level. Among the content ones—in high schools, environmental literacy seems to be on a permanent back burner, issues of race and of cultural identity more broadly remain incredibly hard to discuss, and media literacy is an area where language-arts teachers can feel they are perpetually behind their students. Among the skills issues, levels of both writing fluency and reading or viewing sophistication vary enormously, even among a highly selective incoming population of undergraduate students like ours at UW.

As originally conceived at Brown University, a primary goal of the Texts and Teachers program was curricular enrichment; the introduction into high school curricula of more challenging texts and topics that would be interdisciplinary, cross-cultural, or innovative in other ways. As the UW program developed, we found our local high school teachers to be especially interested in engaging three areas of inquiry that fell outside of their standard teaching opportunities: environmentalism, film/visual culture, and sociocultural diversity. Surprisingly (for us), many high school language-arts departments, even in the twenty-first century, still seem bound to a very traditional canon of literature while at the same time being less than fully clear about their pedagogical purposes in using these particular texts.[5] While the advent of literary theory and cultural studies have powerfully promoted critical thinking about literature, both trends have often encountered institutional resistance at the high school level and, in part as a result, have had difficulty in translating their goals into well-defined pedagogical practices and measurable skills. As a result, high school teachers are often deeply uncertain about how well their classes are preparing their students for college-level analytical reading and writing tasks.

In establishing Texts and Teachers groups, then, it made sense to have the groups centered in areas where we as university faculty were enacting our own curricular innovations and reshaping our own pedagogical practices. Over the course of a decade, we put in place our three current classes, dealing with environmental literacy, visual literacy, and sociocultural literacy, respectively: Living in Place, Film as Narrative, and Margins and Centers. What these classes have in common is the goal of helping students learn how to read differently—more closely, more self-consciously, more empathetically. Although the various texts we use are "difficult" in different ways (for example, the difficulty of Faulkner's prose versus the interplay of images and narrative in film versus the difficulty of acknowledging racist ideology), we look to build with our teachers a core of shared texts that challenge students' assumptions about how reading works, how they see the issues we discuss, and how literature impacts their social worlds.[6]

One accidental aspect of the program's development here has turned out to be fortuitous. The course number we chose for Texts and Teachers is Comparative Literature 240, a course that satisfies UW's main composition requirement. So writing (and, gradually, visual presentation of information, as well) became a key pedagogical objective. Indeed, we are convinced that growth in reading and viewing and writing skills are inseparable processes. The importance of writing at universities is well known, of course; that's why most of them have composition requirements in the first place. But UWTT provides a rare opportunity for high school students and teachers to experience college-level composition assignments, outcomes, and expectations in their own classrooms, as literary criticism and interpretation are actually taught in colleges (embedded in disciplinary content and given deep historical context while creating higher-level rhetorical awareness). In the film-narrative group, for example, the instructors have collaborated on ways to use daily writing to learn and other scaffolded composition assignments to help the students gain skill through regular low-stakes writing. Students develop an understanding of how to "read" a film and of how the visual grammars of filmic technique can be understood and deployed in an academic context. For the high school teachers, too, this is often one of the first times they have consistently modeled their classes on the specific ways upon how writing is taught at a college level, with profound implications for their ability to better prepare all their students for college writing expectations. Indeed, many of the high school teachers in all UWTT groups pair their spring semester Comp Lit 240 course with another UWHS composition course in the fall to provide a productive yearlong first-year writing experience.

Methods and Aims

What are we trying to do with and for our students, with *our* here meaning the entire student population at a given school? Most of them—at least a majority in most settings—are likely to wind up in careers other than university or K–12 teaching. They are not likely to become literary scholars or language-arts teachers, nor will they read, much less produce, literary criticism in any academic sense. The broader success, into the future, of our educational endeavors in the humanities depends instead on helping shape a literate public—people who regularly read varied kinds of materials on a wide range of topics and who have learned how to respond to what they read in analytical, self-reflective, and critical ways. Those literate readers will also understand the act of reading as something more than recreation (though recreational reading has its own values, to be sure) and instead as a step toward integrating into their public and social lives a reflective engagement with challenging texts by allowing those texts to exert pressure on their personal opinions and values. Impacting the widest possible public audiences, however, also means finding ways to make literary/cultural methods of reading and modes of writing more transparent for general audiences—by which we mean making more of our scholarship *and* our teaching less theory laden, less jargony, and thus more accessible to larger public audiences. That we in the humanities have definable methodologies of reading, rather than just habits, is too often not something even humanities majors realize and can articulate, and this is much less for the students we teach in general education classes or at the high school level.

Besides clarifying our aims and methods, we need also to recognize that bridging the gap for students between high school and college learning is a key step in this process, which means having more frequent and more ongoing conversations with our pedagogical partners in the process at the high school level. Doing this conceptual work can have significant additional payoff as well. As the University of Washington (like many public universities) has shifted over the past decade toward being a STEM-oriented Research 1 university, we find ourselves spending more time and reaching more students with little prior background or even interest in the kinds of literacy that the humanities can provide. But these are students who can *become* interested in our issues and our methods if we can figure out how to convey to them the distinctive value of the techniques we employ and the stakes of reading their worlds in these sorts of ways. These students, regardless of what they do professionally, would be more capable of reading and writing in specifiable ways that have value—to them, to society, and to the general project of creating, interpreting, and preserving knowledge in the humanities.

How do we see our students (in ideal scenarios), both at the high school and university levels, being different by the end of a quarter or a semester, which, as all teachers know, is a terribly short period of time? One key outcome is rhetorical in a traditional sense, although newly clarified and articulated for contemporary students in terms of the media that they experience—how words do what they do, why that matters, why we need to be both precise and careful in how we use them (not, for instance, blindly tweeting). Teaching this well means slowing down, taking the time to read a page or a paragraph thoroughly, but also giving students time to practice and to develop these skills for themselves by diving deeply into the language, structures, and purposes of written or visual texts. For some kinds of materials—public science writing, for instance—that may involve synopsis assignments, having students *map* all or part of specific essays is a first step toward deeper engagement with it. For others—literary narratives or narrative films—it may involve creating for or with students an analytical vocabulary that allows them to break down longer texts into structurally related parts. Not by accident, for instance, do many DVD versions of films or television series now come with chapters—a fact that viewers do not always notice and rarely ponder. These are skills that students can learn by reading well-chosen texts in self-reflective ways but then also deploy in their own writing. Thus, the principles of narrative analysis (Handwerk) are minimalist versions of techniques for writing effectively as much as they are practices of reading.

That first goal is, for us, firmly aligned with the historical and social purposes of the humanities, which we see as fundamentally about teaching our students to be more informed, more thoughtful, more articulate, and more compassionate citizens of a global world. Working through the humanities to help students become more skilled in the sorts of areas on which we focus—environmental, sociocultural, and visual literacy—better prepares them for the lives they will lead, regardless of what professional directions they may pursue. An aspect of this process that the humanities can be particularly good at conveying is sharpening awareness of the affective dimensions of important social issues, of the ways in which emotion and intellect intersect in defining and pursuing human values. Emotion and intellect have to intersect quite self-consciously if students are to mature into tolerant and empathetic advocates for social and environmental justice and to feel themselves as participants in a larger global community whose aspirations they share, and to which they can contribute. This sensibility, in turn, must be grounded in a deeper historical awareness than contemporary education, with its focus on the here and now, often provides but which contributes essential background for our present-day circumstances and deliberations.

One uniquely powerful way that Texts and Teachers works toward this essential purpose is that it enacts and embodies these principles in a "rhetoric of presence" in real time. How often do our curricular programs unintentionally reproduce familiar but timeworn educational systems that perpetuate perceptions of hierarchy, status, or power? Instead, the UWTT classrooms seek to overturn these well-worn grooves and that in itself becomes one of the most powerful texts of all that students learn to read. When they see high school and university faculty sharing expertise, community, and collaboration in respectful ways, it speaks volumes to them about what *thoughtful, articulate, and compassionate global citizens* actually do. And so, in that sense, UWTT doesn't just talk about humanity—or the humanities. It is an embodied practice of teaching and learning that is human at their very core. That is one of the most significant lessons we all take from these partnerships.

Impacts on Student Learning

For high school students, our classes visibly enhance their sense of their own expectations, abilities, and confidence—an outcome consistently reported by high school teachers and confirmed by the standard UW student evaluations given to these classes. Especially for high school seniors, who may have begun to look ahead and to tune out, tackling college-level work is a new challenge that renews their academic engagement and, in turn, reenergizes their teachers. The students benefit as well from curricular convergence, working on writing tasks that are fully comparable with college-level assignments; carefully scaffolded assignments are designed to heighten their grasp of what close reading and critical cultural analysis mean in the humanities and why they are worth doing. Teacher feedback and UWHS surveys confirm that students become more confident about their interpretive, participation, and writing skills, an impact that carries over into higher rates of success and retention at the university level.[7]

Both course materials and our collaborative design work with high school teachers help bring about these results, to be sure. Yet somewhat to our surprise, one of the biggest student effects has come from the back-and-forth visits built into the program design. While all UWHS courses require university faculty observations of and reports on the high school classes, UWTT is unique in how all of us visit each high school class at least once a year, teaching that class as we would on our own campuses. This piece adds to the realness of the equivalence experience for students, but there are three additional advantages: (1) we develop over time a much better sense for what our teachers' high school students are like; (2) our teachers get to see how we deal with specific course materials, including, sometimes, our struggles to present them effectively; and (3) we get feedback from our teachers regarding how their students respond to specific materials and teaching techniques.

Once a year, each high school class visits UW as well, not just sitting in on the on-campus version of the class but actively participating. The impact can be extraordinary. These high school students are excited to interact as peers with their university counterparts and sometimes outperform the university students in that setting in their depth of insight, curiosity, and openness. Joining a university class, even for a single day, helps strengthen high school students' sense that they *belong* in college and that they have the tools to succeed there. It gives them a chance to show that they can participate in high-level discussions about complex literary or cinematic texts. They also gain from these experiences an anticipatory sense of the quicker pace and higher intensity of college-level instruction. As one of the creators of Brown's program, Arnold Weinstein, says, "[W]hen a high school student, especially one without huge college prospects, discovers that he or she can in fact 'handle' a college course, something quasi-magical and unchartable *can happen*. We know so little about the Eureka-moments of confidence and discovery, the can-do thresholds, that take place on the inside, invisible to ALL parties, and I have to think this program is big with them" (Weinstein, unpublished).

Even more powerful is an expanded version of the college visit day devised by Anu Taranath, an all-day event that brings together students from several high schools and from UW (as many as three hundred students) for a daylong series of workshops and group discussions on issues of race, gender, sexuality, and poverty. The symposium expands the notion of "margins and centers" well beyond the literary realm and invites students to consider their lives, communities, and broader nation from multiple angles and perspectives. Sandwiched between large group sessions at the beginning and end are periods where these students break into smaller mixed groups with peers from other schools for discussion, with each subset led by one of the teachers involved in that course team.

Professional Development

Working steadily with high school teachers has given us a far deeper appreciation for how hard high school teachers have to work and for how well they do that work. As a result, it can be very difficult for them to stay professionally current with regard to methods or content or to find time and opportunities to reflect metacritically on the relation between accumulated classroom experience and their own or their school's curricular values and outcomes. It can be even harder for them to reinvent themselves as teachers in ways we all need to do regularly if we want to continue to be successful in the classroom. These collaborations also usefully remind us of how privileged we are in some ways as university faculty—especially with regard to how we dispose of our professional time and the opportunities available to us for professional development. In the words of two of those high school teachers:[8]

> As a high school teacher it is rare for your opinion to be asked. It is rare for the years of education that you received to be looked upon as having value. It is rare to be treated like a professional or even simply an expert in your field. Feeling undervalued is one of the reasons so many teachers leave this profession. The importance of the Text and Teachers program lies not only in its ability to demonstrate appreciation for high school teachers, but also in its desire to use our knowledge to help create better systems of collaboration and education. As a collaborator in the Text and Teachers program for the past five years, it has been an honor to engage with other professionals. To share resources, to actually participate in a university class and then take those techniques back to my classroom, to have a university professor say: "that's interesting, share that with us please." The reciprocal nature of the

Texts and Teachers program has propelled my teaching into areas I always wanted to explore, but did not have the time or space to explore on my own. It has profoundly improved my teaching in this program and also how I teach my other classes. Being able to collaborate with teachers who have very different teaching contexts allows me to see curriculum, teaching techniques, and even approaches to individual students through a variety of lenses. It pushes me to take risks in my classroom and to have conversations that are timely, yet generally considered untouchable for high school students. Most importantly, it has kept me in my chosen profession. Every year this collaboration energizes me as it reminds me that I have value as a high school educator and that my knowledge and expertise mean something. (Horner)

I think the most important element of the collaboration from the student perspective would be "presence." By this I mean the students get to imagine (and participate in) the kinds of engagement (both academic and behavioral) they can expect at the college level. Immersed as they are in the ebb and flow of High School life (and all of its accompanying . . . teenage socio-hormonal drama), I try to be deliberate about crafting a rigorous and complex course of study, as well as cultivating an environment of intellectual behaviors that go beyond merely completing assignments. This increased level of deep engagement can initially be off-putting for young people (especially the ones who sign up for this class believing they have mastered the art of "studenting" and all of its accompanying academic short-cuts). The first quarter is usually spent demonstrating to them that they need to shift from seeing their education as a series of tasks I give them, to understanding how to extend their own thinking BEYOND any constructions they may be handed. Instead of waiting to be told what to do and how any assignment applies to them, they must work to learn how to create the application on their own terms and then demonstrate that to me. (Geary)

We are obviously lucky to have such dedicated teachers as our partners and would stress again that the benefits here for professional development flow in both directions. For us as university faculty, the effects have been equally profound, penetrating into every class we teach. Spending time with high school teachers *and* their students has sharpened our metacognitive grasp of issues fundamental to teaching—selection and sequencing of texts, assignment design, methodological self-awareness, and reading and writing habits and practices.⁹ These benefits seem to us especially crucial for the humanities, a collection of disciplines that have—to our minds—considerably less methodological clarity and certainty than most other academic disciplines, ones that have yet to succeed in conveying to the contemporary public the *value* of the sorts of analytical thinking and writing in which they seek to train their students. For reasons like those that Horner's words above convey, it is our collaborating teachers who keep us going and keep us reinvesting in this program and in our teaching careers more broadly.

Institutional Impact

Worth noting is that UWTT exists in a state with several other options for college-equivalent high school work—among them advanced-placement (AP) classes, as in most school districts, but also a very robust and well-supported community college/regional state university dual-enrollment program, called Running Start.¹⁰ High school teachers value the fact that with UWTT, their student population remains in their schools full time, producing a double advantage. The more obvious gain of UWTT versus Running Start for high school teachers is that they get to continue working with more of their most engaged and ambitious students. Yet one should not overlook the impact upon the general culture of a high school to have these students still *present* as part of their student populations. For the students themselves, there is a further benefit. Dealing with college-level material in a supportive and more steadily interactive high school environment can make the first step into university education easier.

How We Make It Happen: Enabling Conditions

Educator-to-educator relationships are foundational—sponsorship and resources must follow, support, and sustain long-term educational partnerships.

Over the course of almost twenty years, we have learned a great deal about implementing a program like ours—on occasion from our mistakes but productively then, as well. Trying to create UWTT teams from the top down, for instance, whether at the school-district level or even that of principals, is one such mistake. It is in individual humanities departments and individual teachers that one finds allies. Outreach[11] to and conversations with those individuals is the essential first step; meeting with the entire faculty of a prospective department is often the best second step, in part because of the value in having multiple teachers involved at each school. Teachers move on or move up with considerable frequency; this is especially true of the kinds of teachers one would like to involve in a program like this. So having departmental support and potential replacements in mind can avoid disruption to the continuity of the courses in individual schools.

And then there is money. Yes, this takes dollars, as well as time and energy. Fortunately, it turns out that it does not require all that many dollars and requires most of those dollars at intermittent moments of start-up or expansion of a working group. Keeping a program such as this one alive after it is underway has proven, at least in a financial sense, to be relatively easy. Here, we need to signal our appreciation for the two units that have been indispensable for UWTT's continuation: UW's Continuum College and the Walter Chapin Simpson Center for the Humanities. Our Continuum College houses the UW in the High School program, admirably directed since 2009 by Tim Stetter. Linking with them was an accident of history that has turned out to be essential for our well-being. When our first courses were established, we wound up working with teachers already involved in UWHS. As a result, we have, from the start, benefited from the dual-credit setup that contributes tremendously to facilitating high school buy-in. High school principals and teachers recognize immediately the practical value of such courses for their students; they typically have some dual-credit classes underway in their schools or at least know about their existence.

No less significant is the administrative support provided by UWHS staff on matters such as classroom reservations, paperwork, and other logistical matters. Crucial for moments of expansion has been UWHS's steady commitment to funding for teacher stipends and course-development workshops. The design workshops typically take up an entire week—a big demand on teachers' time and one that deserves adequate recognition and compensation. UWHS also provides small annual stipends for those of us involved in the program in our roles as coordinators and participants. We have been equally lucky to have received steady support from UW's Walter Chapin Simpson Humanities Center, its director, Kathy Woodward, and the succession of associate directors and staff who have amiably and enthusiastically fostered our efforts—from the development of new collaborative groups to follow-up workshops on topics such as assignment design, evaluation of writing, discussion of rubrics, and grade norming. Individual academic departments, especially UW's comparative literature, cinema, and media department and its English department, have also provided support and encouragement. Overall program coordination is provided by the director of Texts and Teachers, who receives no additional compensation for this role, but the role rarely takes much work except in the occasional years when we put a new teaching team together.

With regard to practical implementation, we have borrowed from Brown's model by preceding every new course with a weeklong summer workshop that brings together the course coordinator and all of the teachers involved. We begin with a topic and typically an idea for a "paradigm text," an initial reading or film that can thematically set the stage for the class as a whole *and* introduce to students the specific reading, viewing, and discussion skills that they will be cultivating throughout their course. We avoid, however, having much else set in stone. The teachers themselves suggest, review, and select texts, aiming with each course for about 70 percent overlap in all participating classes while leaving some room at the edges for individual insertions and changes. We discuss in these workshops the general aims of a humanities curriculum and the ways that this new course might contribute to those. We share experiences about our quite different institutional settings—sometimes the first time that individual teachers have had extended conversations as specific as these about curricular and pedagogical issues with active teachers from other school settings. We talk about the transition from high school to college, with its varied intellectual, social, and psychological difficulties. We discuss constructing syllabi, especially the importance of sequencing texts effectively and linking them across the trajectory of an entire course. We begin the hard detail work of imagining assignments and projects that might best fulfill our course purposes.

This slow work of designing a new course together forms the backbone of our courses and the foundation of our collaborative partnerships in UWTT. It is when fellow educators sit side by side during a summer morning, figuring out together which text or which scene will be the central one in some particular subsection of the syllabus, that real friendships, respect, and collegiality begin to emerge. Early in the workshop, the UW faculty member brings a basic draft or skeletal outline of the proposed course, along with a range of possible texts, assignments, and outcomes. Over the next several days, a collaborative course design grows out of that rough blueprint as each individual teacher's course gets "built out." Through discussion and debate, we define the learning goals of our overlapping courses in different weeks or units and how best to meet them. Different instructors may agree on the goals for a given week while still choosing different texts or assignments for achieving them.

Although texts are shared across institutional settings, creation of assignments and syllabi (sequencing of texts) is left to individual instructors. Yet, even without required parallelism, we find assignments converging as we discuss how to design and refine them. Central to the Living in Place class, for instance, is a focus on literary and cultural texts as arguments—in the sense of not just of offering a stance about the situations they represent but also of being constructed in step-by-step ways that need to be analyzed closely if one is to understand the persuasive impact of a given text. In practice, this means that early assignments focus on very short bits of text, demarcated by the instructor and read with careful attention to the immediate context within which they appear. Turning points in texts, for instance, provide ideal sites for intensive analytical papers that are meant to address the "what," "why" (stakes), and "how" of a given text.[12]

This preparatory work is tremendously valuable, yet it may be the ongoing follow-up and dialogue among all of us that adds the most to our pedagogical awareness. These subsequent sessions can be large or modest. They range from something as simple as a spring debriefing or a fall planning session to full-scale workshops and retreats, but they bring us together in our groups in a way that provides for regular sharing of pedagogical experiences and questions. The Margins and Centers group, for example, meets a few times a year for curriculum workshops, debriefing sessions, and general teaching check-ins. We also gather for three-day retreats where we share stories and cook food together, all while discussing our pedagogical craft. These retreats prioritize relationship building and collaboration among group members within a broader structure of problem solving, retooling, and learning. Because we forge bonds and learn collectively, we know we are upending the standard model of top-down professional development and creating something new. As we strengthen our teaching and mentorship of students, we also create avenues for overworked and underpaid high school teacher colleagues to feel cared for and nourished as valued educators.[13]

How Long Can It Last? Reflections Past and Future

Long-term sustainability rests on administration that values and supports both innovation in learning and effective, visible public partnerships.

Many, perhaps most, efforts at educational reform tend to separate curricular innovation and pedagogical implementation, as if these intricately interwoven aspects of teaching were neatly divisible. UWTT operates from the contrary conviction: that the most effective classroom transformations grow out of *sustained* reflection and interaction among a set of professionals working on shared, classroom-specific pedagogical questions and engaging in the collaborative reshaping of their own curricular and educational practices. Sustaining a program like this one over decades, however, is not a simple feat. There is an invisibility about such on-the-ground efforts for most higher-level administrators that hampers their continuation. Impact is hard to quantify, especially without funding for intensive assessment. Change in personnel creates a host of low-level issues in some years, and the succession of participants needs to be kept constantly in mind—hence the value of having more than one teacher involved at any participating school. Engaging faculty, especially tenure-line faculty, at universities where reward systems rarely take into account these sorts of activities is another significant hurdle; replacing those who cease can be even more difficult.

A larger issue is that scaling up a program like this one can seem exponentially harder than keeping it afloat. The role of director involves considerable (though also intermittent) time making and fostering contacts with individual high schools and humanities departments. The Brown summer workshop model, though, has proven exemplary for creating group cohesiveness. As we have noted, the seemingly accidental advantages we have encountered over time have, in effect, proven essential; not all of these are likely to be replicable at other institutions, though different opportunities may well exist there. And yet, we would argue that following in the footsteps of Brown's initiative is a worthwhile goal, and that sparking similar initiatives elsewhere is possible—indeed, more than possible, necessary, because it offers an instance of how to reformulate the purposes of the humanities in a time when we badly need new initiatives.

We dedicate our final words here to our high school teachers, for whom our admiration is boundless. They are the ones who have provided vital energy and enthusiasm, even in moments when the future of the program seemed uncertain. They have helped convince us of how badly high schools (not all of them, to be sure; some high schools are way ahead of us with regard to curricular transformation) desire curricular change in the humanities and have given us real support in implementing it—sometimes against active local resistance. Despite the much greater obstacles they confront in their teaching lives and settings, they have put their own vitality and creativity into the well-being of this project. We thank them for the pleasure of learning alongside them.

Notes

1. For the 2017–18 academic year, for instance, UWTT enrolled 465 total high school students across seventeen different classes in six different high schools, about half of them signing up to earn official UW credit. In Washington State, the term *dual credit* includes all models in which high school students can potentially earn both high school and college credit through the same course. Information about dual enrollment (a more widely used term than *dual-credit*) programs nationally can be found at the Web site of the National Alliance of Concurrent Enrollment Partnerships (NACEP), which is the national association of colleges and universities (and others) partnering in these programs, and also the accrediting body for this specialized program (http://www.nacep.org/). Their Web site also includes a rich sample of scholarly research on these programs (http://www.nacep.org/research-policy/research-studies/) and a resource page (http://www.nacep.org/resource-center/).

2. In the late 1980s, Arnold Weinstein was asked by Brown University dean of the college Harriet Sheridan to come up with possible models for curricular reform, especially in the area of new horizons and new partnerships. The earliest model, supported by NEH funds and called Great Books Then and Now, consisted of interdisciplinary, team-taught courses at Brown—almost always bringing East–West perspectives and materials into comparative conversation. The teaching component of this program was no less experimental. A number of Providence and rural Rhode Island high schools were brought into the mix; those students frequently attended Brown courses, and Brown faculty visited/taught at least once or twice a semester at many of the regional schools. The later iteration of these concepts was Texts and Teachers, codirected by Arnold Weinstein and Edward Ahearn, also funded by the NEH. It existed during the mid-1990s as an ambitious national effort to define the conceptual parameters of the program and to expand its professional reach. The highlight of Texts and Teachers consisted of two years of summer seminars at Brown, where *teams* of university and high school teachers came to Providence to work with Brown faculty in the preparation of two such courses: Rites of Passage and Desire and the Marketplace. The sites included Seattle, Washington, Memphis, Tennessee, Chicago, Illinoise, and Columbus, Ohio. These teams of teachers committed to constructing their own joint courses, involving intense collaborative work across university and college populations (teachers and students), going forward. Over time, once the NEH funds dried up, there was still modest continued collab-

orative work in Rhode Island for about a decade but full-scale continuation only in Seattle.

3. As just one example of this continuing separation, the NEH Humanities Connections Programs fund grants for curricular development separately in *either* a planning *or* an implementation category.

4. The Washington State Common Core Standards are in some ways admirably specific, yet, at the same time, they are written at a level of abstraction that does not necessarily provide much practical guidance for high school teachers about exactly what to teach, much less how and why, in any precise or detailed ways. The reading standards have us in a world where analyzing themes and topics still seems to be the primary analytical challenge (although they do provide helpful detail about analyzing form and rhetorical or stylistic choices). The standards continue to stress (again without specifying any content) the importance of studying the canon (called "foundational texts"). The writing standards also offer considerable detail about filling out arguments yet with no discussion at all of what constitutes an appropriate or distinctive claim for literary/cultural studies. One major step forward, though, is that these standards now include mention of literary nonfiction. Also good is their stress upon the *comparative* nature of literary/cultural analysis, a crucial methodological premise that all of us share.

5. Despite significant changes in recent years, the advanced placement program continues (at least from the perspective of the teachers with whom we work) to be linked closely to a still-conventional, even if slowly-shifting, canon of the Arnoldian "best" literary and cultural texts and a limited repertoire of strategies for how to read those texts well.

6. Core texts for Living in Place include *Encounters with the Archdruid*; *Robinson Crusoe*; *Go Down, Moses*; *Wild Seed*; and *Ceremony*. Core texts for Film as Narrative include selections from three film studies textbooks, *Casablanca*; *What's Up, Doc?*; *The Searchers*; and *Moulin Rouge*. Core texts for Margins and Centers include *What Night Brings*; *Bastard out of Carolina*; *Grass Roof, Tin Roof*; and *Funny Boy*.

7. UW's Continuum College produces annual longitudinal assessments, most recently for the 2015–16 school year (which had 525 responses). These surveys are not specific to UWTT classes, but individual comments from participants fill out a broad numerical picture about the impact of UW's dual-credit classes. Scores from 2017–18 UWTT high school class evaluations on the Challenge and Engagement Index (a standard item on UW student evaluation forms that combines measures of difficulty with students' perceived involvement in a given class) ranged from 4.5–4.9 (on a 7.0 point scale). These numbers are comparable to the CEI scores from versions of comparative literature or English department first-year composition classes on the UW campus.

8. The first quote comes from Rachelle Horner, who has taught since 2008 at Eastlake High School in the Lake Washington School District, and who currently serves as head of the Humanities department there. The second is from Dan Geary, a teacher at Henry M. Jackson High School in the Everett School District, who has worked with UWHS since 2001.

9. As one instance of the pedagogical tools that have emerged out of the UWTT experience, we include here Gary Handwerk's guidelines for close reading:

Principles of Narrative Analysis (Or, What Good Readers of Literary Texts Read *For*):

I: *Principle of Narrative Economy*—"Every Word Matters"
II: *Principle of Narrative Juxtaposition*—"Location, Location, Location"
III: *Principle of Narrative Coherence*—"Everything Fits . . . But Some Things Fit Better Than Others"
IV: *Principle of Narrative Completeness*—"Now You See It . . . Now You Don't."

10. Running Start is a statewide program that allows high school juniors and seniors to take some or all of their classes on the campuses of nearby two-year colleges and/or regional state universities (https://runningstart.org/).

11. *Outreach*, we realize, can be a contested term with its potential implications of center-out, top-down, one-way curricular enrichment. As we hope our chapter indicates, these are outcomes our program is explicitly designed to avoid. Yet this initial step of making contact with language-arts departments, individual teachers, and often school principals does very much involve actively "reaching out" to create the groundwork upon which we can build stable collaborative pedagogical partnerships.

12. Some program materials are visible online at the Simpson Center Web site.

13. These benefits have become all the more valuable for us in the time of COVID. Over the past year, all of us shifted on short notice to virtual teaching, a transition where our already established interpersonal conversations and slowly acquired collective wisdom about how to teach better in this format have proven tremendously useful.

Works Cited

Geary, Dan. Unpublished talk.
Horner, Rachelle. Unpublished talk.
Running Start. "What We Do." Running Start, https://runningstart.org/. Accessed 6 Mar. 2021.
University of Washington. "UW in the High School." *UWHS*, www.uwhs.uw.edu. Accessed 7 Feb. 2021.
Walter Chapin Simpson Center for the Humanities. "Texts and Teachers." University of Washington, https://simpsoncenter.org/projects/texts-and-teachers-0. Accessed 5 Feb. 2021.
Washington State Common Core Standards. "English Language ARts Standarts." *Corestandards*, http://www.corestandards.org/ELA-Literacy/. Accessed 7 Feb. 2021.
Weinstein, Arnold. Unpublished talk.

Lifting the Color Curtain with the Clemente Course in the Humanities

Jim Cocola

In Worcester, Massachusetts, as academic director and poetry instructor of the local branch of the Bard College Clemente Course in the Humanities, a program providing low-income adults with a multidisciplinary course of study in the liberal arts, I work with diverse cohorts of learners, planning a curriculum staging core elements of the humanistic tradition for a representative cross-section of humankind. Over eight months and one hundred and ten contact hours, students complete coursework in US history, art history, critical thinking and writing, literature, and philosophy. Books, childcare, tuition, and transportation are provided free of charge, and students are eligible to earn up to six college credits for their efforts in the course. We are funded and supported by a combination of organizations and institutions, from commonwealth benefactors like Mass Humanities to private foundations such as the Alden Trust, and colleges and universities, including Anna Maria College, Bard College, Becker College, Assumption College, Clark University, the College of the Holy Cross, Worcester State University, and Worcester Polytechnic Institute (WPI). Other partners include local arts and culture institutions such as the Worcester Art Museum, the Worcester County Poetry Association, and the Worcester Cultural Council, as well as community centers, non-profits, and social service organizations like Ex-Prisoners and Prisoners Organizing for Community Advancement (EPOCA), the Worcester Community Action Council, and Worcester Interfaith.

For Earl Shorris, who founded the Clemente Course in the Humanities in New York City in the 1990s, the aim of the course was "to bring the students into the public world, to take them from the isolation of poverty to the political life of citizens" (118). Over the last two decades, even as the public sphere has shifted toward increasingly virtualized discourses through remediations transforming popular notions of the social, and even while the educational marketplace has shifted increasingly toward online and hybrid modes of delivery, the dozens of Clemente Courses that have emerged around the country have remained dedicated to face-to-face encounters built around the public consequences of humanistic inquiry. If large portions of twenty-first-century scholarship in the humanities happen in closed quarters, on screens, in forms largely distributed by, for, from, and to stakeholders at increasingly privatized institutions, then Clemente represents a space where the humanities still happen by, for, from, and to the public.

Designed around the so-called Western canon as a point of departure toward engaged citizenship, we enlarge that canon in Worcester since we work with particularly diverse cohorts. Such diversity has been encoded into Worcester's urban fabric for generations. The Worcester Regional Research Bureau emphasizes the immigrant dimension of Worcester's diversity, describing it as "a Massachusetts 'Gateway City,'" which "has welcomed residents from diverse backgrounds for decades." But whereas, "prior to 1950, most new residents were born in or descended from European countries . . . since 1950, the city began to attract greater numbers of residents from South America, Africa, and Asia" ("Changing City" 1). Meanwhile, in recent years, Massachusetts has welcomed over two thousand refugees per year, with Worcester welcoming more than twice as many as any other city in the commonwealth, serving as one of the most important places of refuge on the eastern seaboard.

In other parts of the commonwealth, and around the country, many branches of the Clemente Course serve specific city neighborhoods, or, narrower, more homogenous demographics, as for example in Dorchester, on the one hand, or in Springfield, on the other. Meanwhile, in Worcester, we serve all corners of the city, bringing together students and instructors who hail from the four corners of the world. Consider figures 1 and 2, featuring a conversation in a typical Clemente session involving participants with individual or familial roots in Algeria, Italy, Jamaica, Kenya, Liberia, Paraguay, and Trinidad. On this evening, we were reading *The Epic of Gilgamesh*, an ancient text from Mesopotamia re-discovered in the late nineteenth century after two millennia of obscurity, and only recently anthologized in earnest as a centerpiece of world literature.

Lifting the Color Curtain with the Clemente Course in the Humanities   93

Figure 1. Poetry session on *The Epic of Gilgamesh*, February 25, 2016. *Source*: Hannah Coombs.

Figure 2. The Bard College Clemente Course in the Humanities, Worcester, Massachusetts. *Source*: Hannah Coombs.

In his 1979 lectures on *The Epic of Gilgamesh*, Gregory Corso held that "we're all Gilgameshes," but some of our Clemente students don't see it that way. Although many engage primarily with the character of Gilgamesh, as the epic itself and most of its contemporary readers have done, other students pay equal attention to Gilgamesh and Enkidu, and still others find themselves identifying more decisively with Enkidu, coming, as they do, from the social margins and the underclass. Met with Corso's argument that "we're all Gilgameshes," and considering the universal appeal of the titular hero, one student in this year's course whispered, not quite under her breath: "No, we're all Enkidus." Such articulations of class solidarity have been relatively rare among Worcester Clemente cohorts, where students have generally proven quicker to address points of difference constellating around gender, national origin, racialization, religion, and sexuality than to confront their common socioeconomic disadvantage.

Initially this surprised me; now I see it as a revealing symptom of the broader twenty-first-century US aversion to frank discussions about class conflict and social stratification. In fact, Clemente instructors, by their mere presence, can sometimes stand as a bar to such discussions. I have a distinct sense that one of the best conversations at the intersection of classed, gendered, and racialized identity occurred precisely because it unfolded in my absence: we were considering a passage from Claudia Rankine's *Citizen: An American Lyric* (2014), and one of the students explained that it would be easier to discuss the stakes of the passage if I was not in the room. Without missing a beat, I excused myself, explaining that I would be back in ten minutes. When I returned, one of our elder students, a pastor, originally from Liberia, appeared to be moderating a pitched discussion involving differential access to representation in legal matters, which had somehow circled back to an earlier dialogue in our philosophy strand involving Immanuel Kant. I did not inquire as to the arc of what I had missed, and we moved on to the next poem. One lesson here would seem to be that differently configured publics will produce different kinds of conversations and dialogues, resulting in different kinds of action and different kinds of scholarship.

In his apology *The Western Canon* (1994), Harold Bloom defined and defended the canon as "the choice of books in our teaching institutions," even while conceding that "reading the very best writers—let us say Homer, Dante, Shakespeare, Tolstoy—is not going to make us better citizens" (15–16). Perhaps not, though choosing books with attention to literary tradition *and* contemporary communities gives us a better chance, while extending beyond mere reading and into conversation and dialogue among citizens and noncitizens improves our chances further still. Over the course of an academic year in Clemente, in the midst of working from Socrates and Sophocles to a range of modern painters, philosophers, and poets, we consider several figures who have come from the social margins and the underclass, including Richard Wright (1908–60), often hailed among the most accomplished African American authors of the twentieth century. Celebrated for his debut novel *Native Son* (1940) and his memoir *Black Boy* (1945), Wright's literary career evolved in other directions in the 1950s, during a period of exile in France, when he travelled widely across Europe, Africa, and Asia, turning from fiction to poetry and reportage. In 1955, Wright visited Bandung, in Indonesia, where leaders from emerging nations in Africa and Asia gathered to determine their collective future. Wright wrote about this experience in *The Color Curtain: A Report on the Bandung Conference* (1956), reflecting on the racially charged atmosphere at the first gathering of representatives from a set of newly independent African and Asian nations.

During his remaining few years, particularly in work finally collected four decades later in *Haiku: This Other World* (1998), Wright pursued an aesthetic standpoint more closely aligned to African and Asian than to American or European thought. While Wright's turn to haiku can be understood as a mimicry of European American writers like Jack Kerouac, who had been drawn to Japanese forms in the immediate wake of the US occupation of Japan, it can also be seen as a separate errand that flowed from his journey to Indonesia. If, for Sachi Nakachi, Wright's haiku stand as "a product of his colonial ambivalence" (159) and "a Western application of an Asian literary form" (160), they also register as a product of anticolonial solidarity: a shift by an African diasporic away from European and American literary forms occasioned by extended exposure to African and Asian ways of life.

Wright first learned of Bandung while living in exile in northern France, where he recalled reading in a newspaper of "twenty-nine free and independent nations of Asia and Africa" that were "meeting in Bandung, Indonesia to discuss 'racialism and colonialism'" (*Color* 11). For Wright, this was not a gathering of special interests but rather "a meeting of almost all of the human race living in the main geopolitical center of gravity of the earth" (12). Taking place apart from and beyond European and American power structures, Wright concluded that this "meeting of the rejected" was "in itself a kind of judgment upon that Western world" (12) insofar as "the agenda and subject matter had been written for centuries in the blood and bones of the participants" (14). There is a sense in which our Worcester Clemente sessions, too, constitute a "meeting of the rejected": a dynamic that becomes particularly palpable in our US history sessions, where "the blood and bones of our participants" (12) matter deeply to the arc of our discussions.

These discussions aren't always easy, for a mix of philosophical and pragmatic reasons. We always see things from different perspectives, and we sometimes struggle to make those differences plain to one another. Nevertheless, we do our best to deal with communication challenges mirroring those that Wright foresaw at Bandung, where he anticipated that "the English language was about to undergo one of the most severe tests in its long and glorious history" (*Color* 200). Poised as English was to become "the common, dominant tongue of the globe," it followed for Wright that "soon there would be more people speaking English than there were people whose native tongue was English" (200). In Worcester Clemente, this ratio does not always pertain, but on some nights it does, with many struggling more decidedly to formulate sentences in their second, third, or fourth language of English than they do to formulate ideas in their first language, which may not be comprehended by anyone else in the room.

Whether their expressive English ensures active participation from the start or limits their contributions until midyear or later, Clemente students in Worcester enter with baseline standards of receptive English and receive broad exposure across the pillars of the so-called Western canon. However, they also gain awareness of materials extending beyond that tradition and consider these in counterpoint, whether measuring the Parthenon against the Pyramid of Djoser and the Great Zimbabwe or the sonnets of William Shakespeare and Philip Sidney against those of Wanda Coleman and Terrance Hayes. In the process of encountering such works, they encounter each other, with interpretations of artistic, historical, literary, and philosophical narratives verging into narratives of their respective lives. Both kinds of work are salutary. "We have to write our own stories," Vicky Mireles, a 2015 graduate, argued in one of our class sessions, "and our own histories. No one is going to write them for us. You're never going to find these things in the books" (Mireles). What our students do find in the books speaks volumes about the books and the students alike. Yes, we read and write on the classics, and on counterpoints to the classics, but we also read and write each other.

Books figure into our work, but we ourselves figure into our work just as centrally—in a work that also includes many other kinds of texts. Our classes are held in the Worcester Art Museum, which allows our art history instructor to conduct multiple gallery tours throughout the academic year. Moreover, our proximity to the American Antiquarian Society (AAS) ensures that Clemente students are able to engage material from an unrivaled archive of early US print culture whose broadsides, manuscripts, newspapers, and other print materials read quite differently among this cohort than among the general run of AAS fellows, members, and patrons. With this background to draw upon, Clemente students can better appreciate Wright's haiku not only as a publishing phenomenon but also as an archival phenomenon, for among the four thousand haiku Wright wrote in the last eighteen months of his life, very few made in into print over the next four decades. In fact, three thousand of them remain unpublished still, confined to manuscripts held in the Beinecke Library at Yale University.

Like all texts, books speak differently to different students. On the occasion of his September 2016 public reading at WPI and his appearance at the first Worcester Clemente session of the academic year, the words and works of visiting poet Martín Espada resonated especially strongly with our Puerto Rican students but also appealed to those who had experience with the legal system. It is one thing to speak about rights in the abstract, or, even more particularly, with respect to the arguments of John Stuart Mill and Karl Marx, and quite another to consider them in view of a personal narrative such as Espada's poem "Mariano Explains Yanqui Colonialism to Judge Collings." While my WPI students might struggle collectively to explain the relationship between Mariano's "¡Pa'l carajo!" and the interpreter's "yes" (*Alabanza* 45), my Clemente students collectively read this short poem across multiple registers, from English to Spanish and from the logics of the courtroom to the logics of mass incarceration. Meanwhile, Espada's poem "Return" touched a nerve with one of our Brooklyn-born students, linking poet and listener alike to "the dim angel of public housing" (*Republic* 45)—a phenomenon that could by appreciated if not wholly understood by those of us who spoke without Brooklyn accents.

In the following September, when Naomi Shihab Nye held a public conversation at the Worcester Art Museum and made an appearance at the first Worcester Clemente session of the academic year, she shared poems not only by her own hand but also by the hand of her late father, Aziz Shihab, himself a Palestinian refugee who had left unpublished work behind in his notebooks. In one of those poems, "Many Asked Me Not to Forget Them," Shihab asks, "How much do I think of Africa?" before expressing his sadness over "places I didn't / have enough energy to worry about" (33). Looking around the room, our students recognized Shihab through his daughter's channeling, seeing in each other people who had also been forgotten, and who came from places many lacked energy to worry about.

As a public, the Worcester Clemente cohorts emerge from specific—and profoundly complex—class positions, but also from specific—and profoundly complex—geographies. In this regard they reflect their city, whether Worcester is for them a place of recent arrival, long residence, or multigenerational affiliation. In an annual session on Worcester poets, where we invariably read Elizabeth Bishop's signature Worcester poem "In the Waiting Room" alongside other local landmark poems from Stanley Kunitz's "The Portrait" and Charles Olson's "The Thing Was Moving" to Diana Der-Hovanessian's "Hometown" and Christopher Gilbert's "Now," students are consistently captivated by works deeply embedded in the fabric of the city. The poems are hyperlocal in their references, invoking dentist's offices, football stadiums, neighborhoods, parks, restaurants, and surrounding towns that conjure strong associations. In 2015, we were joined at this session on Worcester poets by Cheryl Savageau, a writer of Abenaki and French Canadian background whose kinship to Worcester and to the Native histories of the region helped our students rethink their mental maps of city and nation alike. In her poem "Looking for Indians," Savageau reframes New England from an Indigenous perspective, while "Department of Labor Haiku," with its "winter snow" and its "men out of work" (53), links to Wright's work and to our ongoing dialogue about class positions and social identities. With Savageau in the room, we considered the more impersonal trajectories of industrialization and postindustrialization through discussions of labor that simultaneously intersected with gendered and racialized dynamics.

In 2016, in conjunction with the session on Worcester poets, and together with the sponsorship of the Worcester County Poetry Association, we held a reunion reading of the Worcester's Free People's Workshop, active in the late 1970s and early 1980s, in honor of its late convener, Etheridge Knight, and Christopher Gilbert, his sometime deputy, which featured readings and reminiscences by John Hodgen, Cheryl Savageau, and David

Williams. How astonished Williams was to arrive early to the event, held at the Worcester Public Library, only to encounter a group of twenty-odd strangers discussing his poem "Breath"! As he entered the room, Clemente students were trying to discern the nature of the poem's speaker, descended from people "thrown away / as if they were nothing" (5). Williams has Lebanese descent lines, but most students weren't aware of this biographical detail before he emerged among them, nor did they realize that the poet himself was hovering at the edge of their conversation. While some of those born in the United States wanted to locate his work in the deeper histories of transatlantic enslavement, more recent immigrants to the United States preferred to read the poem in connection with a broader and more contemporary set of experiences marking the exile and the refugee. And there was Williams, listening to the churn of both readings.

Here was an example of literary criticism in public, en route to scholarship as manifested in student essays and in this chapter alike. But what makes such public work scholarship, and what makes this scholarship public? By Timothy K. Eatman's definition, public scholarship manifests itself in "scholarly or creative activity that joins serious intellectual endeavor with a commitment to public practice and public consequence" (18). In the Worcester branch of the Bard College Clemente Course in the Humanities, this activity produces faculty and student intellectuals in the mold that Julie Ellison describes as the "positional humanist," poised to "mediate between one place and another and between one kind of practice and another" (294). These mediations occur constantly in Clemente: between ancient Mesopotamia and contemporary United States; between neighborhoods and between continents; between oral and written testimonies; between personal narratives and argumentative essays, all of which pivot back to the practices of our students, in view of the consequences that such work entails.

Whether casual reader, college student, or professional scholar, it is one thing to consider a literary work in solitude—or as close to solitude as we might come in such individual acts of reading—and quite another to do so in company. I have touched elsewhere on the dynamic of spatialized collective reading in my chapter "*Dutchman* in the Round," which elaborates my teaching practices connected to Amiri Baraka's *Dutchman* (1964), where I emphasize the virtues of "turning the classroom into a theatrical space where instructor and students are interpellated on a pedagogical stage" (34). In Worcester Clemente, as at WPI, my classroom conversations and dialogues tend to unfold in circles, but even when there is no one performing in the middle of that circle, everyone is performing at its perimeter, for we perform our readings for each other, to each other, with each other in mind. Think, for example, of Bishop's lines from "In the Waiting Room": "you are one of *them* / *Why* should you be one, too?" (150). The speaker in this poem, at once six and sixty-five, asks these questions to herself, as does the reader who considers them privately and silently. But to read these words aloud in company is another matter entirely.

For this reason, whatever the company, I always prefer that short poems—and, at the very least, selected lines from longer poems—be read aloud more than once, on the conviction that any public will give different kinds of hearings to different kinds of speakers. Here, I point not only to the fictive speaker that separates herself from the poet on paper, but also to the human speaker that gives that fiction a voice in the company of a classroom. What kind of company? How do listeners affiliate or disaffiliate from the various speakers that emerge therein? "You are one of *them* / *Why* should you be one, too?": as I listen to and speak these lines again each year with a new group of Worcester Clemente students, they raise questions about the pronouns we use to invoke, affiliate with, and distance ourselves from one another. Why me, or us, apart from them? Why with *them*? Why not? And for what reasons? Bishop's lines can be activated along the axes of class, gender, nationality, and race, among others: for some of our students, they resonate in all of these keys, and beyond.

Bishop, like many of our students, spanned various locales across the Americas in her life, but our students tend to come in equal numbers from the African and Asian diasporas. As such, our program connects to students from initiatives that include the Higgins School of Humanities at Clark University and the Latino Education Institute of Worcester State University, as well as to key members of local non-profit and social services organizations such as the African Community Education Program and the Southeast Asian Coalition. Because Worcester, as the second largest city in New England, at just under two hundred thousand residents, is large enough to foster an array of partnering entities and initiatives but small enough that constituents from said partners might come together under one roof, we have resisted hitching our star too closely to any one of them. We receive faculty stipends and other operating funds from arts and culture enterprises, colleges and universities, and local foundations. We receive neighborhood spaces in which to hold class sessions, community dinners, commencement ceremonies, and other outreach activities from churches, libraries, and museums. We receive student referrals and support services from commonwealth, federal, and private charities and cultural affinity groups. We would not flourish to the extent that we do if we lacked support from any one of these key partners.

Taken together, in all of their diversities, our annual cohorts comprise a series of miniature Bandung Conferences of their very own. In coming together to contemplate their relationship to US citizenship, or the lack thereof, students and instructors in the Worcester Clemente Course also come together to contemplate their relationship to the wider world, much as leaders like Zhou Enlai of China, Sukarno of Indonesia, and Gamal Abdel Nasser of Egypt came together at Bandung in 1955 to contemplate their respective national interests in the context of the wider world. If Wright took it upon himself to contemplate the consequences of the Bandung Conference, then our respective iterations of Bandung take it upon ourselves to contemplate not only the consequences of works by writers like Wright, but also the consequences of our collective contemplation itself. In this regard, teaching Wright in the Worcester Clemente classroom allowed me to see his work in ways that were not nearly as apparent in my WPI classrooms, which have relatively high percentages of international students by some metrics, though certainly not in comparison with Worcester Clemente cohorts. In both cases, I prepared to teach Wright's work with reference to the poems themselves and to the scholarly conversation about them; in the context of Worcester Clemente, I returned to said poems and to said scholarly conversation with an enhanced sense of the poem's audiences and contexts, which is to say, the poem's publics.

Wright's turn to haiku in the final years of his life is sometimes read as an isolated aesthetic decision but can also be read as part of a larger shift toward Asian cultural forms. This shift also marked the late work of UN Secretary-General Dag Hammarskjöld, whose posthumously published memoir *Markings* (1963) was written in his first language, Norwegian, taking the form of a prose narrative interspersed with a series of haiku. Wright's turn to haiku also bespeaks a realignment of African American culture toward Asia in the second half of the twentieth century. This shift was routed in part through the catalyzing influence of Baraka. As Michio Arimitsu observes, Baraka's poetic allusions to Asia "symptomatically revealed the deep psychological conflicts about his own marginalized racial identity while complicating the black-and-white dichotomy of race relations in the

United States" (81). For Baraka, the shift came early as late, from his collaboration with Hettie Jones on the co-edited journal *Yūgen: A New Consciousness in Arts and Letters* (1958–62) to his late experiments in *Un Poco Low Coup* (2003), which inflected Japanese precedents through the jazz influence of Bud Powell in order to produce the "low coup," an American form mutually indebted to Africa and Asia. Following Wright and Baraka, several other Black poets have prevailed upon Japanese forms such as the haiku and the tanka. In 1985, Etheridge Knight published a series of "Black Man Haiku," which remain uncollected; more recently, there are the examples of Sonia Sanchez's *Morning Haiku* (2010) and Harryette Mullen's *Urban Tumbleweed: Notes from a Tanka Diary* (2013).

Wright's *Haiku: This Other World* begins with a poem that may well be his most important haiku of all:

I am nobody:
A red sinking autumn sun
Took my name away. (1)

This printed instance departs from two earlier printed instances of the poem, all three of them posthumous. The first instance, printed in an *Ebony* feature of 1961, shortly after Wright's death, reads:

I am nobody
A red sinking Autumn sun
Took my name away (Harrington 92)

The second instance, printed in 1978, offers the same version, except for the minor restyling of "Autumn" as "autumn" (*Richard Wright Reader* 253). The changes to this poem made in *Haiku: This Other World* might appear largely cosmetic, involving matters of lineation with respect to the margin, on the one hand, and details involving punctuation, on the other. Yet the lineation helps to temporalize the lines in relation to one another, locating "a red sinking autumn sun" at an earlier point, while the punctuation reinforces the poem's causal relationship, with the colon underscoring the cause-and-effect relationship between the poem's first lines and its last two lines.

Asking "Can Black Art Ever Escape the Politics of Race?" Vinson Cunningham recently held up Wright's haiku as an example in the affirmative, arguing that they focus not on politics or race, but rather on "the sublimity of nature, the ultimate momentariness of human life, the tenuous and uncountable associations that hang between phenomenon and perception" (Cunningham). While a phenomenological reading of Wright is certainly possible, Worcester Clemente students tend to read Wright's "I am nobody" not as a nature poem but rather as a comment on enslavement, placing adjectives like "red," "sinking," and "autumn" within the space of the middle passage. I take their readings as a refinement of Wright scholar Yoshinbou Hakutani's assertion that this poem "suppresses subjectivity by depicting the red sun that erases his name" (141). In fact, the name isn't erased but rather taken away, in an appropriation that does not look to efface but rather to exploit. It is not the poem that suppresses Wright's subjectivity but rather the historical conditions that occasioned the poem. Hakutani proceeds to argue that "the poet is strongly present, even by negation" (141): more specifically, a negation structured by the shadow of a stolen name. While I could pass off this engagement with Hakutani's reading as my own literary analysis, it represents a strand of my scholarly activity that could only have emerged in community, and in public.

As my Clemente students have helped me to understand, this haiku's *muga* (無我), or non-selfhood, paradoxically emerges through the predicament of Black subjectivity in exile. Wright—for we cannot yet call him by another name in the absence of the one that has been stolen—subtly contends with the legacies of enslavement from a transatlantic vantage point. In their afterword to Wright's *Haiku: This Other World*, coeditors Hakutani and Robert L. Tener style the setting of this poem as "a vague place in autumn" (277), but a considered biographical and historical reading can posit a more precise location for the poem and the poet—namely, in Normandy, looking westward across the Atlantic, where Wright re-enacts the trajectory of the middle passage by following the trace of the sun. If, for Lucien Stryk, a haiku's *muga* activates "so close an identification with the things one writes of that the self is forgotten" (16), then, for Wright, the self is not so much forgotten, but rather found as lost, at once asserted and negated. The pathos of this plight emerges in a sunset recalling the path of those forbears reduced from personhood to thinghood by their enslavers. In elliptically recalling those humans who were rendered as things, Wright's person simultaneously emerges even as it finds itself resubmerged.

The kigo (季語), or seasonal reference, also bespeaks the legacies of enslavement, with Wright's "red sinking autumn sun" pointing not only to the western horizon but also to the Western harvest, whose origins center upon plantation economies enabled and fueled by the enormous exploitation of the enslaved. As Sachi Nakachi argues, Wright's self-representation as "nobody" belied his literary celebrity, minimized here by his implicit identification with "the thousands of nameless Africans who sank in the bottom of the Middle Passage while a red autumn sun beamed overhead, or those slaves who had to work relentlessly while a 'red autumn sun' sank into the West." (179–80). Such identifications had structured Wright's work since *12 Million Black Voices: A Folk History of the Negro in the United States* (1941), a collaboration with photographer Edwin Rosskam. Wright began this work by writing that "each day when you see us Black folk upon the dusty land of the farms or upon the hard pavement of the city streets, you usually take us for granted and think you know us, but our history is far stranger than you suspect, and we are not what we seem" (10). So, too, with Wright's late haiku, easily taken for granted and thought known but far stranger than one might suspect. The strange history of Black folk might seem absent from these brief poems, but Blackness stands as the very ground on which Wright's Japanesque figures have been written.

When read in isolation, a dislocated and unattributed phrase like "red sinking autumn sun" might carry a melancholic tone seeming primarily seasonal in its affective impact. However, when read in the context of this poem, the set of poems from which this poem springs, and the life and work of the poet who wrote it, the phrase emerges as a powerful instance of the Black signifier, a string of "words with demonstrably African American referents" (Cocola, "Multimodal Encounter" 140). Though not as direct as proper names such as Langston Hughes's "Harlem" or Maya Angelou's "Killens," Wright's "red sinking autumn sun" offers an implicit gloss on African American history nevertheless, even as it points to the circumstances of a Japanese empire in eclipse.

I'm not sure I would have made the connection outside of an multidisciplinary teaching opportunity devoted to parallel forms of inquiry in art history and in poetry, but I have been struck by the fact that Wright's "red sinking autumn sun" also converges with the red sinking autumn sun of J. M. W. Turner's painting *Slavers Throwing Overboard the Dead and Dying, Typhoon Coming On* (1840), more recently known as *The Slave Ship* (see figure 3). Turner's painting depicts the *Zong* massacre of November 1781, when, en route from Liverpool to the Caribbean, running low on provisions, a British crew massacred over one hundred enslaved men, women, and children and threw them overboard with the intention of collecting

Figure 3. J. M. W. Turner, *Slavers Throwing Overboard the Dead and Dying, Typhoon Coming On*, 1840. Oil on Canvas, 35.7 in. × 48.3 in. *Source*: Museum of Fine Arts, Boston.

insurance claims upon arrival in Jamaica. Here, as in Wright's poem, we have ample evidence of the sunset, together with more oblique suggestions of the enslaved and massacred. Turner himself, also a poet, had evoked the massacre as early as 1812, in his poem "Fallacies of Hope," setting the event amid "angry setting suns and fierce-edged clouds" (Finberg 474). Elsewhere, the most sustained literary treatment of this event, Tobagonian Canadian poet M. NourbeSe Phillip's fragmentary, book-length work *ZONG!* (2011), relies on the atomization, blurring, and deferral of language in the telling, offering its own hauntingly and inevitably elusive account of transatlantic enslavement through the prism of the *Zong* massacre.

Tracing this literary history to its root, in what can be understood as a crucial catalyzing event for the movements and works that followed from it, Olaudah Equiano brought the matter of the *Zong* massacre to the attention of Granville Sharp, one of the most active British abolitionists of the eighteenth century, leading Sharp to articulate "the Necessity of putting an entire stop to the Slave Trade" (qtd. in Faubert 1). Though I had read

Equiano and Philip, and though I had seen Turner's painting, I did not route all of these intertexts through Wright's haiku until reading it in the company of Clemente students from Ghana, Liberia, Jamaica, Trinidad and Tobago, and the United States, who put pressure on—and prompted me to put a different kind of pressure on—every single one of the dozen words in the poem.

Red. Sinking. Autumn. Sun. Upon further reflection, I see in "red" and "sinking" not only the characteristics of the sun, but also the lineaments of the enslaved, massacred, and drowned, in Turner's brushstrokes and Wright's language alike. Thanks to the insights of Clemente students, I recognize the omissions that mark Turner's painting and the poems by Wright and Philip, where so much of what remains undepicted stands at the very center of the matter. "Perspective," Wright argued in his early essay "Blueprint for Negro Writing" (1937), "is that part of a poem, novel, or play which a writer never puts directly upon paper" (*Richard Wright Reader* 45). While reading Wright's work more carefully and thoroughly has helped me to discern elements of that perspective, doing so in the company of Clemente students—working as and working among fellow positional humanists—has also been crucial to these efforts.

Thanks to Clemente students, I also recognize that Wright's poem isn't simply a question of the African diaspora. Clemente students born in or with familial ties to China, Korea, and Vietnam are as likely to equate a "red sinking autumn sun" with China, Japan, or the Soviet Union as with the United States or West Africa. Like transatlantic enslavement, the globalizations and globalized conflicts of the twentieth and twenty-first centuries have done a great deal to create nobodies and to take names away. It was through Bandung that Wright came into a fuller lived consciousness of this fact, and it has been, among other experiences, through my work in Clemente that I have done so. My sense of what counts as public and my sense of what counts as scholarship have been forever changed in consequence.

One of our Clemente students, reduced by his wartime displacement in childhood, retains only the vaguest sense of a birth date, a birthplace, or a given name. He has only one picture of himself from childhood, taken at a refugee camp in Thailand: a photo that became the subject of his Clemente essay "I am Number 4." When this student encountered Wright's haiku, he did so as a reader of Asian origin displaced to the United States by a conflict between American and Asian forces, reading poems penned in Europe by a writer of African descent and American origin. This student undertook his reading in the company of fellow students with African, American, Asian, and European origins. And so, sixty years and more after Bandung, the Worcester branch of the Clemente Course in the Humanities provides a site where the color curtain might be lifted, however fleetingly, bringing together those from diasporic communities of various origins in a commonly held site of exile, and linking them with others born and raised here, working together from a common dwelling place.

Such community building comes in part thanks to considered discussions of works like *The Epic of Gilgamesh* and Wright's haiku. These discussions, in turn, occasion modes of collective action and literary criticism informed by the complex challenges and responsibilities of conducting scholarship in public. While such dynamics are flourishing at dozens of Clemente Course branches around the country, in the wake of the economic crises occasioned by the COVID-19 pandemic, new branches and connections are needed now more than ever before. Although the possibilities for in-person engagement remain uncertain in the immediate term, the shift to remote learning has opened various possibilities for virtual connection, linking publics across substantial geographical divides. Those interested in joining the work of the Clemente Course—whether connecting to existing branches or starting new branches of the Clemente Course in their own rights—can begin the process by contacting Vivé Griffith, the national director of outreach and engagement, and by engaging the staff of their state humanities council in order to gauge commitment and support for such an initiative.

Whether students in our local Clemente Course have been affiliated with Worcester for months, decades, or generations, my impression of many of them echoes Wright's impression of the delegates at Bandung, who, "for the most part, though bitter, looked and hoped toward the West." For Wright's part, he felt that "the West . . . must be big enough, generous enough, to accept and understand that bitterness" (*Color* 201). At the same time, he understood the risks undertaken by those that pursue projects in the humanities. Speaking in the week after the Bandung Coference in an address to an Indonesian audience titled "The Artist and His Problems," Wright recalled the murder of his friend Louis Adamic, noted Aristotle's sentiment that "literature is dangerous work," and encouraged "young writers" to "enter the political arena, go in search of glory and money, but don't be surprised if you end up losing . . . your head!" (qtd. in Roberts and Foulcher 133). Within five years, Wright was found dead in Paris, in circumstances that some have construed as murder. Twelve years later, Sukarno, the first Indonesian president, was deposed in a violent upheaval killing as many as a million or more, and was subsequently placed under house arrest, where he died three years later.

There are some who would redirect initiatives like the Clemente Course away from all canons, in order to teach a more heterogeneous curriculum that better reflects the makeup of their student cohorts. For his part, Shorris envisioned the Clemente Course as a curriculum poised against "official, acceptable interpretation" (111), valorizing the humanities as a tradition which, "contrary to the views of some critics of what they refer to as 'the canon' or the works of 'dead white European males,'" tends to center on "the works of troublemakers, artistic and intellectual dissidents, those who were both critics and builders" (225). That said, the barriers of Eurocentrism and white supremacy remain, and we do not overlook them. Nor do we overlook troublemakers or dissidents of color: many of these number among our favorite authors, while others number among our finest students. In my seven years of affiliation with the Clemente Course, I have reached the conclusion that canons and counter-canons are most effectively read and understood when taken together. In Worcester, we lift the color curtain not to pretend that it doesn't exist, or to stand on one side of it, but to look across the larger scene, as an audience that is always already on stage. While diversity and inclusion in the classroom and on the syllabus form critical aspects of our mission, contending with the expressions and representations—the truths, lies, facts, and opinions—found in the diffuse tradition that travels under the heading of "Western civilization" also plays an integral role in the work that we do. We work through the bitterness that such work entails, in order to better look and better hope—not toward some idealized or sanitized version of "the West," but toward each other.

Works Cited

Abdulgani, Roeslan. *Bandung Connection*. Translated by Molly Bondan, Gunung Agung, 1981.
Arimitsu, Michio. "Playing the Dozens on Zen: Amiri Baraka's Journey from a 'Pre-Black' Bohemian Outsider to a 'Post-American Low Coup' Poet." *Traveling Texts and the Work of Afro Japanese Cultural Production: Two Haiku and a Microphone*, edited by William H. Bridges IV and Nina Cornyetz, Lexington Books, 2015, pp. 79–98.
Baraka, Amiri. *Un Poco Low Coup*. Razor, 2003.

Bashō. *On Love and Barley: Haiku of Basho.* Edited and translated by Lucien Stryk, U of Hawai'i P, 1985.

Bishop, Elizabeth. *Poems, Prose, Letters.* Edited by Lloyd Schwartz, Library of America, 2008.

Bloom, Harold. *The Western Canon: The Books and School of the Ages.* Riverhead, 1994.

Cocola, Jim. *Dutchman* in the Round: *Approaches to Teaching Baraka's* Dutchman. Edited by Matthew Calihman and Gerald Early, The Modern Language Association, 2018, pp. 34–41.

———. "Multimodal Encounter: Two Case Studies in the Recovery of the Black Signifier." *Poetry and Pedagogy across the Lifespan: Disciplines, Classrooms, Contexts,* edited by Sandra Kleppe and Angela Lee Sorby, Palgrave Macmillan, 2018, 139–61.

Corso, Gregory. Lecture on the *Epic of Gilgamesh.* Jack Kerouac School of Disembodied Poetics, Naropa University, Boulder, CO, 1 Jul. 1977, https://archive.org/details/Gregory_Corso_class_1_July_1977_77P091.

Cunningham, Vinson. "Can Black Art Ever Escape the Politics of Race?" *The New York Times,* 20 Aug. 2015, https://www.nytimes.com/2015/08/20/magazine/can-black-art-ever-escape-the-politics-of-race.html.

Der-Hovanessian, Diana. "Hometown." *Forkroads: A Journal of Ethnic-American Literature,* vol. 6, 1996, p. 64.

Eatman, Timothy K. "Engaged Scholarship and Faculty Rewards: A National Conversation." *Diversity and Democracy,* vol. 12, no. 1, 2009, pp. 18–19.

Ellison, Julie. "The New Public Humanists." *PMLA,* vol. 128, no. 2, Mar. 2013, pp. 289–98.

Espada, Martín. *Alabanza: New and Selected Poems 1982–2002.* W. W. Norton, 2004.

———. *The Republic of Poetry.* W. W. Norton, 2006.

Faubert, Michelle. *Granville Sharp's Uncovered Letter and the Zong Massacre.* Palgrave Macmillan, 2018.

Finberg, A. J. *The Life of J. M. W. Turner, R. A.* 2nd ed., Clarnedon Press, 1961.

Gilbert, Christopher. *Turning Into Dwelling,* Graywolf Press, 2015.

Hakutani, Yoshinobu. *East-West Literary Imagination: Cultural Exchanges from Yeats to Morrison.* University of Missouri Press, 2017.

Hammarskjöld, Dag. *Markings.* Faber and Faber, 1963.

Harrington, Ollie. "The Last Days of Richard Wright." *Ebony,* vol. 16, no. 4, Feb. 1961, pp. 83–94.

Jones, LeRoi. *Dutchman* and *The Slave.* Harper Perennial, 2001.

Knight, Etheridge. "Black Man Haiku." *Mickle Street Review,* vol. 7, 1985, p. 50.

Kunitz, Stanley. *The Collected Poems.* W. W. Norton, 2000.

Mireles, Vicky. Interview. Conducted by Ousmane Power-Greene, 21 May 2015.

Mullen, Harryette. *Urban Tumbleweed: Notes from a Tanka Diary.* Graywolf Press, 2013.

Nakachi, Sachi. "Richard Wright and the American South." *Richard Wright Writing America at Home and From Abroad*, edited by Virginia Whatley Smith, UP of Mississippi, 2016, pp. 167–83.

Nye, Naomi Shihab. *Transfer*. BOA Editions, 2011.

Olson, Charles. *The Collected Poems of Charles Olson: Excluding the Maximus Poems*. Edited by George F. Butterick, U of California P, 1997.

Philip, M. Nourbese. *ZONG!* Wesleyan UP, 2008.

Rankine, Claudia. *Citizen: An American Lyric*. Graywolf Press, 2014.

Roberts, Brian Russell, and Keith Foulcher, editors. *Indonesian Notebook: A Sourcebook on Richard Wright and the Bandung Conference*. Duke UP, 2016.

Sanchez, Sonia. *Morning Haiku*. Beacon Press, 2010.

Savageau, Cheryl. *Dirt Road Home*. Curbstone Press, 1995.

Shorris, Earl. *Riches for the Poor: The Clemente Course in the Humanities*. W. W. Norton, 2000.

Williams, David. *Travelling Mercies*. Alice James Books, 1993.

Worcester Regional Research Bureau (WRRB). "The Changing City—Starting a Conversation." Bureau Brief 14–04, Nov. 2014, http://www.wrrb.org/wp-content/uploads/2015/06/WRRB-Bureau-Brief-The-Changing-City-November-2014.pdf.

Wright, Richard, and Edwin Rosskam. *12 Million Black Voices: A Folk History of the Negro in the United States*. Viking, 1941.

Wright, Richard. *The Color Curtain: A Report on the Bandung Conference*. World Publishing, 1956.

———. *Richard Wright Reader*. Edited by Ellen Wright and Michel Fabre, Harper and Row, 1978.

———. *Haiku: This Other World*. Edited by Yoshinobu Hakutani and Robert L Tener, Arcade Publishing, 1998.

Dancing with the Inductive

The Emergence of a Centre for Community Engaged Narrative Arts

Daniel Coleman and Lorraine York

In his compelling study *Why Indigenous Literatures Matter*, Daniel Heath Justice describes the urgent importance of stories for Indigenous peoples who have survived, and who every day continue to survive, colonialism. Stories can be, he acknowledges, "agents of both harm and healing" in that they can be used to "separate" and disconnect in a world where "disconnection is cause *and* consequence of much of this world's suffering," but they "can be good medicine too. They can drive out the poison, heal the spirit as well as the body, remind us [Indigenous peoples] of the greatness of where we came from as well as the greatness of who we're meant to be" (4–5). Justice's observations are specifically addressed to Indigenous folks whose stories have at times been drowned out by harmful colonialist stories *about* Indigenous peoples. In contexts such as these, oral narratives can be a means for marginalized communities to circulate "good medicine" in a way that bypasses officialdom's avenues of cultural production. In his invocation of stories' capacity to extend or deny connection, Justice highlights how stories' power to forge collectivity (whether in the direction of expansiveness, solidarity, or exclusion) is one that can be perceived in any number of human—and for that matter, nonhuman—communities. As scholars and teachers of Canadian literatures, we have devoted a good deal of our lives to this truth, but we have recently been reminded of just how various and profound the relationships between communities and stories can be.

Almost three years ago, in response to an invitation from the faculty of the humanities to propose new research centers, a group began to form around the idea of community and story and to brainstorm what eventually became McMaster University's Centre for Community-Engaged Narrative Arts (CCENA). In this chapter, we trace the development of this center and the various choices we made, regarding everything from terminology (*community-engaged*; *narrative arts*) and philosophy (arts-based; community-initiated), to modes of operation (methods of sharing projects) as we proceeded under the wise counsel of our group of advisors and interlocutors. Drawing upon a rich archive of projects that CCENA has nurtured and facilitated over the past two years, in this chapter we will explain (1) our decision to defer our definition of the center's key terms *community engagement* and *narrative arts*; (2) our development of a meeting format, the *long table*, which is indebted to the community practice of the feminist artist and theorist Lois Weaver; (3) our preference for a community-engagement model that seeks ways to accompany and support already-ongoing community initiatives rather than launching our own; and (4) our decision to cede academic expertise over and ownership of the projects that we supported, to let go of our specialized research fields and venture into what we didn't know. Ultimately, to stray from the deductive, dance with the inductive.

In embracing induction, we knew we were straying from many aspects of the academic mindset that had been carefully inculcated in us over many years, particularly the notions of mastery and specialization, though in other respects, as we shall explain, we were extending and paying tribute to some of the methodologies and conditions of traditional scholarship in literature and the humanities. But in embracing the unknown, and being content in the initial stages of the center's existence to *not* know what defined the center, we came to understand that we were working within a framework of *evolutionary learning*. Rather than leading with a definition of the center's commitments, and thereby circumscribing and predetermining what activities would "fit" under its institutional aegis, we listened to and learned from what community members and advisors brought to the table. In that spirit, this chapter shares what we have learned about "community-engaged narrative arts" from the projects and thinkers with whom we have had the good fortune to work.

Founding CCENA

We begin, fittingly, with narrative: the story of how CCENA came to be. The faculty of the humanities call for proposals was, in the first instance, a call to apply for seed funding that might eventually lead to the establishment of a research center. At McMaster, as at other Canadian universities, our faculty of humanities has tended to produce fewer research centers than the faculties of science, engineering, health sciences, business, or the social sciences, and our dean was eager to redress this imbalance by, first, seeing if the current activities of faculty members might contain the seeds of viable centers for the future. Initially, we saw this call for funding as an opportunity to provide junior colleagues of ours and emerging community-based research centers with research assistants (RAs) to support their projects, all of which engaged in some way with community knowledges and histories. What this meant in practice was that we were able to distribute funds to hire seven graduate-student RAs to support various colleagues' projects, which ranged from studies of the narratives and archives of mixed-heritage people of Chinese descent in late imperial contexts (Hong Kong, Liverpool, and London) and children's interpretations of creation stories on the Six Nations of the Grand River reserve (Canada's most populated reserve, just a half-hour from campus) to the sorting and cataloguing of archival materials repatriated from the Smithsonian Institution to a new archive on Six Nations to queer organizing against gentrification in the city of Hamilton. We now realize that we were able to think in the first instance of supporting our colleagues' research because of the particular conditions and traditions of humanities scholarship that allow for relatively dispersed nodes of scholarly activity. That is to say, we could enable knowledge-generating scholarship by distributing the seed-grant monies to colleagues who were working in a number of areas rather than needing to concentrate activity and resources in the research lab—the model common to knowledge production in the sciences, health sciences, and engineering. The existing conditions of research in the humanities therefore dovetailed with our developing sense of not needing to "own" the research that we support. In retrospect, then, our redistribution of this seed grant was a model for what CCENA's work with community-based projects would become.

Our humanities training, and our individual histories in the academy, though, also left us with a complicated legacy when it comes to articulating how CCENA's collaborations constitute "scholarship." Lorraine, as an emerging scholar in the 1980s, entered a Canadian English department that was, almost to a person, deeply resistant to the new intellectual movements sweeping the North American academy: continental post-structuralist theory and the political interventions it enabled by activating the variables of class, gender, sexuality, race, and ability. She was enormously excited by these new theories of textuality and their implications for a literary study animated by the desire for political justice, but quickly registered that many of her male, British-trained senior colleagues sought to devalue those theories by associating them with a development of which they brusquely disapproved: the growing professionalism and increased emphasis on publication that they dubbed American-style "research" in contrast to their leisurely, genteel and gentlemanly "scholarship." And that "scholarship" was decidedly a product of the isolated, individual scholar-gentleman's private study: no community, no politics invited. She decided that if "research" were the alternative to "scholarship," then she would, faute de mieux, produce "research." Fast-forward to an institutional moment over two decades later, when Daniel, in a volume he coedited with Smaro Kamboureli entitled *ReTooling the Humanities* (2011), identified "research" as a distinctive product of an early twenty-first-century neoliberal regime of university organization that "privileges the culture of research capitalism" (7)—that is, measurable metrics of productivity; extracted, commercialized knowledge; and the consequent, constant pursuit of external research dollars. In fleeing mid-twentieth-century "scholarship," had we run headlong into the arms of "research capital"? And, if we are caught up in its arms, what does that entanglement bode for collaborative community work of the sort that CCENA intended to take up? How could we not need to "own" the projects we promoted, if we were operating in a corporatized milieu that privileged the ownership and extraction of research capital? It soon became apparent, even this early, that if the center were to survive the experimental, tentative phase of its existence, we would need to dance ever so dexterously between the legacies of "scholarship" and "research."

At the end of the seed-grant period, we were invited to submit a proposal for a research center, and because we both happened to be Canadian literature specialists, we initially thought that we would reflect those interests in the proposed center, perhaps by forming a center focused on Canadian literary culture. However, as the projects previously mentioned indicate, many of the people we wanted to work with did not see themselves reflected in the term *Canadian*, either because their work was not focused on Canada or because *Canada* signified a colonizing state apparatus with which they did not identify. And as for the term *literature*, we were reminded by our group of interested cothinkers that it would leave out many media in which storytelling and narrative take place: film, theater, visual art, Indigenous wampum studies, and much more. We therefore downplayed the label *literature* in order to regain the essence of the literary that matters most to us: to trace and enhance the mutual nourishment of communities and stories. We knew we wanted to see how a research center could facilitate the capacity of communities to make compelling stories and for those stories, in turn, to make "beloved communities" in Martin Luther King Jr.'s sense of the term—communities based on equity, justice, reciprocity, and mutual respect (58). Exploring these intuitive interests with our team of advisors, the title Centre for Community-Engaged Narrative Arts gradually emerged as a more inclusive option. As a result, we found ourselves productively distanced—or, at least, positioned aslant—from our specific fields of academic specialization.

By "productively distanced" we mean that disciplinary banners such as "literary criticism," "literary studies," or "Canadian literature" did not align with our desire to generate partnerships with already-ongoing community-narrative initiatives. As we grew to see how these labels excluded the very communities we wanted to work with, we realized that we needed to retool our own training in these disciplines for a broader public environment. So, for example, the literary method of close reading, which, whether in its new-critical guise or in its return to deconstructive theory, exhorts readers to immerse themselves in close attention to the fine-grained details of a literary text, undoubtedly influenced our instinct to listen first to the fine grain of what community groups aimed to do and to then allow our concepts and terminology to emerge from their initiatives. Indeed, we might say that our recontextualized close reading of how communities around us were going about making narratives involved a retooling of another common method of literary studies, reader-response criticism, which asserts that a text's meaning does not inhere in its already-achieved structure but in the page-by-page inductive process of interpretation. Certainly, we felt that our predisposition to hold the shibboleths of our own disciplinary training lightly while we opened ourselves to the terms and priorities that we believed would emerge through reciprocal, practical participation in existing community story-making initiatives accorded with literary studies' ongoing project to engage what Edward Said called *The World, the Text, and the Critic*. We felt the importance of this extra-disciplinary learning in part because of a growing feeling of crisis in our field of English literary studies, where enrollments in the humanities at ours and many other Canadian universities, including in literary studies, are in sharp decline. We have been struck by how many vital and dynamic story- and narrative-making initiatives are emerging in our postindustrial city at the very time that these enrollments are in decline, and we are curious to probe this seeming disconnection, the better to support nascent initiatives in our discipline, such as the growth of community-engaged instruction (in our own department, for example, the introduction of a new course on creative writing in/with/for communities). Thus, we are conscious of how our training as literary scholars has shaped CCENA's starting assumptions, even as we have dropped the categories of literature and the literary from CCENA's defining terms.

As we took those first steps to name ourselves in a way that we hoped would foster rather than forestall collaboration, we experienced the tug of institutional desires and priorities from the university on other levels as well, some of which nourished our thinking and some of which we chose to diverge from. In the former category was an initiative led by McMaster's then incoming president, Patrick Deane. In 2011, he issued a letter entitled "Forward with Integrity," in which he wrote: "rather than relegate community engagement to the status of a 'free floating add on,' something we do on our own time, we need to integrate it fully and meaningfully into the work of the academy—into our normal activities of exploration, questioning and synthesizing, and subject to the most rigorous academic values" (8). We were aware that many publicly funded universities felt a growing responsibility to break down the perceived isolation of the "ivory tower" and to present their work as relevant and vital to wider society, and we were also aware of how the domains of university research that translated most readily into commercialization could be perceived to be most readily engaged, relegating the humanities and arts to noncommunity-engaged frills. Our belief, however, was that narrative or story, thought broadly, was essential to any formation of community, and the question of who tells which stories about which communities was essential to the ethics of engagement.

In sorting out priorities like these, we were undertaking a process of benefitting from some institutional agendas while developing a growing sense of our philosophical commitments to some types of community-engaged scholarly practice and not others. Consulting with other community-engaged initiatives on campus helped us further formulate and commit ourselves to those priorities. The university itself was in the process of establishing the Office of Community Engagement, which was generating a campus-wide strategic plan for community engagement, a community guide to working with McMaster researchers, an online tool to support these kinds of connections, and McMaster's first interdisciplinary class for leaders in community engagement. While we were involved in establishing the Office of Community Engagement (Daniel served on the committee that framed its values and procedures), we decided that our preference was for hands-on work—that is, supporting already-ongoing arts-based-narrative initiatives in communities rather than importing to those communities our sense of how community-engaged knowledge production should look.

In this spirit, we sought to depart from a long history of academics controlling the locus of narrative by means of their access to publication, to credentializing bodies, and to the avenues for mobilizing and commercializing knowledge. So we determined early on that we would try to listen to and support narratives that various communities in our region were *already* generating. We gathered around ourselves people with community links, knowledge, expertise—people who had already thought intensively about community knowledge—and we asked them to serve on our advisory board. People like the editor of a local online magazine of cultural affairs, a gentrification and skateboarding-community activist, the associate director of a neighboring university's Community Engaged Scholarship Unit, the owner and manager of an independent bookstore renowned as a hub for writers and storytellers in the city, the senior project manager for the Deyohaha:ge: Indigenous Knowledge Centre and former special assistant to the director of the Smithsonian's National Museum of the American Indian. We asked these people to join CCENA's advisory committee not only because we had witnessed their community storytelling activities in our city and knew they had cogent insights into and experience in how to *do* community-engaged narrative arts, but also because we knew they were involved in various community networks and they could therefore help us link up with other community-based artists beyond our immediate circuit of acquaintances. Because we were surrounded by people who brought such rich experience to our table, we were all the less inclined to impose our agenda on what community-engaged narrative arts had to be or mean. Gradually, this disinclination became a foundational philosophy of CCENA: a thoroughgoing commitment to evolutionary learning. By *evolutionary learning* we do not mean the kind of flatly teleological, positivistic development that a popular sense of the term *evolution* might call to mind.[1] Instead, we understand the term *evolution* to encompass multiple routes to learning, be they trajectories, reversals, detours, meanderings. Accordingly, evolutionary learning, for us, means resisting paradigms that imagine success as the immediate grasp of concepts—a paradigm that is deeply embedded in Euro-Western narratives of epistemology (think Archimedes's "Eureka!"). Instead, evolutionary learning is slow learning: a patiently attentive feeling of comfort with being suspended in a condition of not knowing and a trust that research directions, definitions, and results best emerge from the resourcefulness that is (always) present in any community.

Indeed, the very first events that CCENA sponsored were experiments with the principles of evolutionary learning. We held two panels that asked participants: What does "community-engaged narrative arts" mean in the worlds in which you live and work? Our wise advisory committee members counselled us to devote our first panel to "narrative arts" and the second to "community engagement" rather than the other way around; "community engagement" had by then become such a widely retailed institutional buzzword that we thought beginning with the more capacious and unbranded "narrative arts" might allow us to begin expansively. Asking community-engaged participants to tell us what narrative arts meant to them, and listening to their responses, took us further than we could have ever imagined, from the importance of listening before narrating to the decentring of a human-centric model of storytelling. In a decisive move away from the deductive, our dance with the inductive opened us to the possibility of the land itself telling its stories.

Precedents for the Establishment of CCENA

Looking back through the lens of evolutionary learning, we can see how several key experiences had prepared us for the process of inductive consultation. In 2011, a year before the seed grant that launched CCENA, McMaster's Anti-Poverty Action Committee proposed that the university offer a free Humanities 100–style course for people in the region who had faced barriers to postsecondary education. Daniel was asked to design the first course. The committee brought in the directors of three programs at other universities that had been largely modelled on the Clemente program, which offers courses in Great Books of Western Civilization, commonly in poor inner-city neighborhoods, to empower disadvantaged people with knowledge of the European canon and also to increase their confidence in their own learning and ability to communicate (for more information on the Clemente approach see Shorris). Guided by the good minds of the Anti-Poverty Action Committee, we then met with focus groups of potential inner-city students in our city to see how the course might be organized. Daniel's training as a literary scholar inspired him to think of proposing a course on Writing Hamilton in which he and the students would read poems, fiction, and creative works about our own city (rather than the canons of Western literature, as in the Clemente program) and then ask students to try their hands at writing one of these forms. Hamilton is known for being the hub of Canada's steel smelting and its many affiliated forms of manufacturing and production, but the decline of the steel industry in the 1980s and 1990s created a unique matrix both of poverty, since many people had lost their manufacturing jobs, and of remarkable artistic productivity, since empty warehouses offered inexpensive studio spaces for a wide range of artists and creators. So the time was ripe for a class that brought these phenomena together. Writers and artists were engaging in manifold ways with Hamilton's "rustbelt" experience, and those who had been dumped from a now-outdated economy had compelling stories to tell. We had assumed that writing would be a good way to tell these stories, but our focus-group meetings with potential students included people from a brain injury clinic, new immigrants to Canada, and people living precarious lives in shelters. They helped us see that not everyone would be able to produce literary writing. So we retooled our plans and called the class Voicing Hamilton: History, Art, Expression. Students would study a broader range of forms—including works of photography, poetry, film, history, and visual arts—about the city by artists and writers who live there. These artists and writers in various media and genres would then visit the class, meet with the students, and help them get started on their own works, from photo essays and urban-history mapping to documentary films and short stories. The focus groups informed us about where to hold the class (near the central bus station), when (on Saturdays), how many students to enroll (not more than twenty-five), how much reading to expect each week (enough to be challenging but not so much as to interfere with other responsibilities such as jobs and parenting), how to support those with children and elder care, when lunch should be held (between the two-hour morning and afternoon sessions;

food was very important—see our discussion of the long table below!), and so on. This experience of having community members' priorities and needs shape the content, scope, and sequence of the class, and the incredible buy-in from students generated by this approach, plus the multimedia and cross-genre understanding of what constitutes narrative art, set a precedent in our thinking for how important broad and diverse consultation would be to the formation of CCENA. So when it came time to establish our center, we began to assemble the advisory committee, mentioned previously, of community- and university-based people who could form a diverse focus group to guide our thinking about priorities, methods, and themes.

A second previous experience also played a key role in shaping our inductive approach to establishing CCENA. In 2007, a group of Indigenous leaders and McMaster professors met to establish a new community-based research center at Six Nations Polytechnic on the Grand River Territory of the Haudenosaunee just a half-hour drive south of McMaster University. The elders who offered us their advice suggested that the Indigenous Knowledge Centre be called Deyohahá:ge:, which means "Two Paths" in the Cayuga language. The idea was that this center would bring together the best of Haudenosaunee knowledge, ways of living, and being with the best in Western methods and epistemologies to construct a research hub on Indigenous territory to benefit the Six Nations community. Daniel served on the steering committee, and the experience of listening to the priorities and plans of the lively group of researchers on the reserve, some of whom were also McMaster researchers and some of whom were full-time on the reserve, presented a model of listening to community priorities. It helped us stay alert to how universities can extract knowledge from communities in ways that alienate their knowledge from its origins, even as it helped us see how universities can provide important support and infrastructure to enable community-led and -owned research to thrive. The Haudenosaunee are some of the most "anthropologized" Indigenous peoples in the world, both because they live in the Northeast of North America and thus had the longest contact with incoming Europeans, and because their traditional territories around St. Lawrence and upstate New York meant they were local to many of North America's earliest university institutions. Indeed, it is widely held that anthropology as an academic field of study emerged with Lewis Henry Morgan's *League of the Ho-De'-No-Sau-Nee, or Iroquois*, published in 1851 (Monture xi). Over the long history of seeing their traditional ceremonies, spiritual practices, and knowledge not only misrepresented in academic research but also used to limit and restrict their sovereignty, Six Nations people, like many other Indigenous peoples, have become vigilant about the provenance and scope of research: Who designs the project? Who decides what its priorities should be? Who benefits from any funding? Who owns the knowledges that result? With considerations like these in mind, it was very important that the Grand River community take precedence in answering all of these questions. That is why its staff, directors, administration, and its physical location are all based on Six Nations territory. Working with these Indigenous researchers and being conscious of the actual *location* of scholarly work also put place- and land-based learning on our radar, reminding us of how the narratives that enable particular knowledges to emerge and thrive arise in social and environmental contexts that remain integral to their applicability and influence. We learned that "community" need not be restricted to human communities alone.

Finally, a third influence shaped our growing understanding about what community engagement could be and what values might guide CCENA. After completing her PhD, one of our former doctoral students, Elizabeth Jackson, had gone on to do postdoctoral work at McMaster's Institute for Excellence in Teaching and Learning where she studied the current literature on community engagement and interviewed staff at research and teaching centers across Canada that focused on university-community relations. Her resulting report went on to guide McMaster's development of their Office of Community Engagement. In that report, *Community-University Engagement in Canada: Voices from the Field* (2014), she noted that several "[k]ey ideas that emerged repeatedly included: mutuality; agency; access; responsibility; and social change or social justice" (5–6). She placed emphasis on these values by citing one of her interviews on one of the priorities that should drive community engagement: "One of them being social justice. Another one being included in the process, in particular marginalized communities, people who don't typically have a voice. So . . . ideally, that's the goal" (6). These priorities dovetailed exactly with our experiences of working with the Discovery Program and with Deyohahá:ge:. Conscious of the history of universities' extractive relationships with communities who serve more often as subjects of study than as designers or participants, we were powerfully drawn by these values, and they became guiding principles as we began to develop relationships with various partners, both on and off campus, who could advise us about what "community engagement" and "narrative arts" might mean.

CCENA's Gathering Format: The Long Table

Those values—especially mutuality and access—also informed our decisions about the format of CCENA gatherings: what they would look and feel like. In the past, we had organized academic conferences that sought to reshape the traditional authority structure of the academic conference (another triangular hierarchy with plenary speakers at the apex, followed by panel participants and listeners) through the use of alternate structures such as combining a day of five- to ten-minute public summaries of research with subsequent days of participant writing workshops (Blair et al. and Tanti et al.). In that spirit, with our CCENA meetings we wished to create a kind of "anti-lectern" effect that would extend hospitality, enact mutuality, and allow knowledge to flow multidirectionally. We called our meetings "long tables" in recognition of that alternative paradigm and, truthfully, because we were struck by the appositeness of the table metaphor to an organization called CCENA—for minus one C, the acronym means "dinner" in Italian and Spanish. What we didn't know at the time, but embraced heartily thereafter, was that the term *long table* had a distinguished feminist genealogy. Lois Weaver, the prominent US queer feminist dramatist, activist, and cofounder of the influential Split Britches lesbian theater collective, coined the term in 2003 to describe a meeting that combines theatricality and public engagement. Weaver was inspired by the 1995 Dutch feminist film *Antonia's Line*, in which the protagonist returns to the small village she was born in and proceeds to construct a feminist utopia there, complete with an expanding dinner table that welcomes all who wish to join her household. (Eventually, the table stretches outdoors!) Like us, Weaver places her dinner/meeting tables in expandable configurations; like us, she envisions this arrangement as providing an alternative to conventional panel discussions that hierarchize expertise. As befits Weaver's artistic practice, her long tables are explicitly performative; they enact "a performance of a dinner table conversation," at which extra tables and spaces can be added as needed. While our long tables are less consciously theatrical, they also seek to transform the experts' panel into the dinner-table conversation, and over food and drink we have experienced illuminating moments when the presenter/listener dynamic has been reconfigured. For example, at a long table devoted to an oral history project about a Hamilton neighborhood called Brightside that was nestled against the Steel Company of Canada's (STELCO) factories until it was almost all bulldozed, several

Figure 1. The long table. *Source*: Lorraine York.

members of the original neighbourhood, who had been participants in the project, were in attendance. Within the expansive spaces of the Long Table, they began to share their own memories of Brightside (see figures 1 and 2).

Indeed, they ramped up the political import of the project when they called for members of city council to be invited to future presentations on the Brightside Project so they would be moved to address the strong currents of resentment that persist to this day over Hamilton City Hall's complicity in the steel company's razing of the neighborhood in the 1960s. This moment of community testimony ensured that the dynamic of the event would not replicate the all-too-familiar paradigm of so-called town hall meetings where experts external to the community propound their visions or plans for that community and ostensibly consult "stakeholder opinion" prior to an already foreseen implementation of top-down planning. Instead, the Brightsiders set the table and collaborated on the menu; as they told their stories, our table expanded.

Figure 2. The long table. *Source*: Lorraine York.

As our long tables expanded, in the sense of growing in number, they brought to our attention philosophies that nourished our understanding of what community-engaged narrative arts might do and be. At our first long table on narrative arts, one contributor argued that listening is a potentially revolutionary act. In speaking about storytelling, she observed, we are often so influenced by the term's conjoining of "story" with "telling" that we neglect the role of listening, and that such neglect can have ethical consequences, for listening is essential to the respectful acknowledgment of the stories of others. Another contributor to that panel picked up this crucial thread, warning us about the tendency to place stories, particularly those from communities whose stories are not as often told, within our own cognitive and ethical frameworks and not those of the storytellers. She asked us to be particularly wary of the reception of stories that casts tellers as "broken" and listeners as "saviors." And a third participant troubled the assumption that just getting people to tell their stories will somehow lead to social justice. These wise reminders dovetailed, in our minds, with the striking call made by the Tuscarora scholar Rick Hill for "knowledge *de*mobilization": a corrective to many non-Indigenous educational and granting institutions' emphasis on an instrumentalization and commercialization of knowledge that ultimately leaves the researcher in a position of sovereign power to apply or circulate knowledge in "the world."

Other philosophies that we imbibed from the thinkers at our long tables similarly challenged taken-for-granted assumptions about stories and communities. One participant shared her experience with what she called, after George Lipsitz, "arts-based community-making" and everyday, mundane acts of improvisation. She showed us what can happen, for example, when a group of teenagers of various abilities go out into a city space and ask passersby, "Would you like to hear a story?" We were inspired by the reversal performed by Lipsitz's phrase "arts-based community-making" of more standard phrases such as "community-based art-making" or, indeed, "community-engaged narrative arts"! As Lipsitz has observed, "[W]hat critics and curators often describe as community-based art making is better described as art-based community making—a form of democratic interaction that enacts the just social relations that social movements often envision" (Estrada n.p.). For example, the project Lipsitz heads up at the International Institute for Critical Studies in Improvisation's center at the University of California, Santa Barbara, Arts-Based Community Making in Black and Chicano Communities, documents "the ways in which improvisatory and other creative activities might disrupt the documented link between discrimination and negative health outcomes" (n.p.). Lipsitz's disruptive coinage captures the spirit of understanding that we at CCENA have incrementally gained from the long tables: that narrative art generates community as much as community generates art.

Another long table participant queried a fundamental assumption about community narrative that we hadn't ever considered when she reminded us that stories are not just oral; they can be performances, images, representations, objects such as wampum, and physical journeys through space, through the land. Why, then, we wondered, as we contemplated the implications of her observation, do we assume that storytelling need be an exclusive property of human animals? Deeply inspired by her questioning, we planned another long table for the following year devoted to this very subject of storytelling of/in the more-than-human world.

Finding Our Principles

In our second year of operation, we followed up these nascent philosophical meditations with a session that sought to bring them to the surface. We devoted a long table to what we might learn from other Canadian groups that have put art-based community making into practice: one from Burnaby, British Columbia; one from Quebec; and one from Vancouver. The first of these was represented by Sarah Schulman, founder and social-impact lead of InWithForward, an initiative started in Holland that is now active in a couple of Canadian cities, including Burnaby and Toronto. This group of community workers radically questions received knowledge about community needs. For example, members of InWithForward offer their labor as cleaners for free to disadvantaged community members. But they are more than volunteer cleaners; they are also conversationalists, philosophers of the everyday, who engage the people they visit in stimulating conversation about larger issues beyond the material questions of what they need to physically survive. In so doing, InWithForward strikingly redraws psychologist Abraham Maslow's hierarchy of needs that sees physical needs like food and shelter as fundamental and needing to be met before pursuing higher-order needs such as intellectual stimulation or creativity. Schulman and InWithForward note that Maslow's hierarchy doesn't align with the way the people they work with identify their needs; often, they cite the "higher order" needs ("sense of purpose," "self-actualization") that appear at the top of Maslow's triangle as primary rather than secondary. Furthermore, they ask, how might it feel to look at needs as not forming a hierarchy at all but as *concurrent*? We at CCENA found this an inspirational corrective to the common assumption that those who do community-engaged work already know what the community's needs are, and it reinforced our determination to take a back seat to the objectives, priorities, and aspirations that communities have already articulated and continue to articulate in their everyday acts of creativity.

Gord Tulloch, director of innovation for posAbilities, a large nonprofit organization in Vancouver, British Columbia, that provides services to people with intellectual disabilities and their families, also emphasized the importance of non-hierarchical, concurrent, and arts-based approaches to addressing community needs. He spoke of how social work as a field started from informal, local attempts to meet the needs of marginalized people, but how the bureaucratic machinery of funders, reporting systems, accreditation, labor contracts, and security protocols that have subsequently overtaken the field tends to bog down agencies' abilities to engage creatively and adroitly with people's needs. The result is that workers and clients find themselves trapped in policies and procedures often far removed from the situations they ostensibly aim to address. No one's life changes with a new coat or a bowl of soup, Tulloch said, if their need for beauty, love, hope, or redemption is ignored. This is as true for the recipients of social services as it is for those who deliver them. He urged social agencies to shift from addressing lower order bodily before higher-order spiritual needs (e.g., housing first, creative outlet second; safety first, flourishing second) to a kind of "both/and" thinking that considers them as interdependent. He noted that changing these approaches to community engagement involves reconsidering the stories we tell and the words we use to describe community challenges, solutions, and futures. Indeed, Tulloch emphasized the importance of art, philosophy, beauty, and narrative in creating not just community but social and political change itself, for it is in the realm of the arts and culture that change becomes possible. "If there's no cultural receptivity," he said, "there can be no political receptivity."

Tulloch's attention to how different words generate different stories is illustrated in Schulman's suggestion that it makes a big difference if those involved in community engagement think of themselves as "workers" or as "experimenters." When they are considered "workers," their efforts become circumscribed by a world of wage labor; the delivery of goods and services; of contracts, products, liabilities; and health and safety, all circulating in a hierarchically organized bureaucracy. If they were considered "experimenters," by contrast, their activities would be more tentative, less pragmatically oriented toward building solutions for people. Indeed, as in scientific experimentation, those involved in community engagement would test hypotheses without the immediate pressure to turn their work into a product or commodity. There would be room for trying things out, testing a possibility, evaluating it, discussing the pros and cons with others involved in the experiment, before consensus grew about the viability and sustainability of the approach. Experimenters are accountable to their team and to the learning process itself, but that accountability should not be precluded by accounting, by foreclosing the process of learning by weighing it against a ledger of deliverables and best practices.

At the same long table, Nadia Duguay and Maxime G. Langlois represented Exeko in Montreal, an agency that experiments with many practical initiatives, including an "intellectual food truck" known as Libre-Library that has crisscrossed Montreal for five years, delivering books and art materials and promoting discussions; critical-thinking "self-defense" workshops on "logical fallacies" for people who have been through the criminal-justice system so they can identify gaps in reasoning and better defend themselves in future; and artists-in-residence programs that cocreate artwork such as murals, choreography, and poetry with citizens on the streets. Exeko's three social innovation labs—the Inclusive Culture Lab, the Inclusive Knowledge Lab, and the Inclusive Speech Lab—pursue research on exclusion and marginalization, in which marginalized citizens are co-researchers and not subjects. All of these activities are based on the belief that encouraging artistic and intellectual creativity is an important part of inclusive and emancipatory social transformation. Considering the violence of intellectual marginalization to be one of society's major isolating forces, Duguay and Langlois spoke of Exeko's efforts to generate what they called "intellectual emancipation," after Jacques Rancière's *The Ignorant Schoolmaster: Five Lessons in Intellectual Emancipation*. For them, intellectual emancipation consists of affirming and enhancing the knowledge people already have and giving them ways to critically analyze what often displaces their knowledge and does their thinking for them. Their experiences with these various initiatives in Montreal have taught them that creative and artistic activities are crucial to the process of intellectual emancipation, especially when those who have been marginalized regain the capacity to tell their own stories, as did at-risk youth on Kanesatake Mohawk reserve on the edge of the city when they worked with Exeko to reestablish their long-defunct community radio station. The long table with our visitors from InWithForward, posAbilities, and Exeko was a truly galvanizing afternoon for all of us at CCENA—hosts, advisory committee members, community researchers, university folks, and general public alike—not only because of the creativity of the three organizations' activities, but also because of the way they affirmed the importance of narrative arts—including poetry, art, music, and philosophy—as crucial tools for looking outside of what we think we know so that we can invent new configurations of community that are built on reciprocity and equity rather than hierarchies of expertise.

As we learned from such inspiring interlocutors about values that we, too, felt to be crucial—intellectual emancipation, the foundational nature of ostensibly higher-order needs, and community leadership in determining objectives—we began, in turn, to articulate those kindred values in other public forums. When we were asked to be the subjects of a short video promoting CCENA on our faculty's website, we saw an opportunity to enunciate our growing sense of these values of intellectual emancipation and cognitive justice (https://www.youtube.com/watch?v=i-z3G8TVaig). Aware of the institutional placement of this video, we gestured both to McMaster-specific discussions and to larger philosophical considerations that transcend the academic setting. As part of our intrauniversity communication, we related CCENA's objectives to McMaster president Patrick Deane's "Forward with Integrity" letter, which we have discussed previously, particularly his precept that community engagement should not become a superficial adjunct to faculty research imperatives. But we went further. Sharing our growing respect for arts-based community making, we pushed the discussion in the direction of social justice and community-devised objectives. Daniel described CCENA's dedication to reaching beyond an understanding of literature as a world unto itself and "thinking more about how narratives become the glue of community-making. Can we help communities attend to those narratives in the way they might want to attend to them?" Such a recalibration of the "criticism" of *literary criticism* repositions the act of critique within a dialogical, collective, and consultative framework, rather than assuming it as the act of the solitary scholar. Lorraine observed that a foundational philosophy of CCENA was cognitive justice, paraphrasing Boaventura de Sousa Santos's striking declaration in *Another Knowledge is Possible*, "There is no global justice without global cognitive justice" (xix). However inductive and mindfully slow our evolutionary learning process may have been (and continues to be), it did not translate into a vagueness about our commitments or a disinclination to articulate them.

Indeed, some of our founding commitments created the context in which we could allow ourselves to trust the inductive process. Key among these was the commitment to place, already implied in the concept of community engagement. Very often the *uni* in *university* assumes a universalizing project, in which researchers aim to produce knowledge that can travel anywhere in a global market. This assumption means that having one's research taken up in far-flung places around the world is seen as proof of success, while research that addresses more specific, local concerns is seen as limited in scope and importance. The unfortunate result is the popular vision of the ivory tower, where the academy's knowledge moves in circuits that seem remote from the daily lives of local people—it's all "academic." This remoteness leads to distrust, since local populations often provide data and research subjects but rarely see the results. For us, making a commitment to place-based scholarship meant a radical experiment in trust: trust that narrative activity in our city was resourceful enough, dynamic enough, diverse enough to reward research that focused on our local region; trust that working outside of our disciplinary comfort zones would lead us to new ways to learn and carry out research; trust that our community partners and advisors would lead us to productive and engaging projects. This trust in place led, in fact, to our inductive method: our commitment to place necessitated an evolutionary process of listening and learning, then improvising and adapting along with the various people we met (and continue to meet) in our community to envision what community-engaged narrative-arts research might be. In a 2003 article arguing for what he calls "critical place studies," professor David Grunewald (now Greenwood) brings together critical pedagogy theory, as developed by Paulo Freire, Henry Giroux, and Peter McLaren, with its focus on social justice and human equity, into dialogue with pedagogies of place, which tend to focus on the environment. Greenwood argues for bringing these two fields together, noting that Freire observed that critical pedagogy emerges from the situation people find themselves in, and that situation is shaped not just by social arrangements but also by the geographical context within which human relations are structured and arranged. Greenwood writes: "Place, in other words, foregrounds a narrative of local and regional politics that is attuned to the particularities of where people actually live, and that is connected to global development trends that impact local places" (3). Here, Greenwood addresses a common concern about place-based approaches—that they will be limited to ingrown, parochial concerns. But, as any good storyteller will insist, the quickest way to the universal is through fine-grained attention to local detail. How can we address global injustices or environmental problems if we cannot attend to and address those we find immediately around us? As any climate change researcher or activist will affirm, concerns about global warming must be addressed in a million specific places. Thus, Greenwood explains, "A critical pedagogy of place aims to (a) identify, recover, and create material spaces and places that teach us how to live well in our total environments (reinhabitation); and (b) identify and change ways of thinking that injure and exploit other people and places (decolonization)" (9). Launching CCENA required a basic trust in our place—in the resources and resourcefulness of our literal location—if we were to engage in a process of listening to and learning from those who were already engaged in creating narratives in our city and beyond.

Our previous work with students in the McMaster Discovery Program and with Six Nations colleagues and researchers at Deyohahá:ge: put us in dialogue with people who never divided the social from the environmental, the local from the global, and this experience—in addition to the aforementioned talk by Dr. Bonnie Freeman, an Algonquin-Haudenosaunee presenter at our very first long table gathering, urging us to include the stories of the land in our research—made us determine early on that our understanding of community-engagement would emphasize a critical engagement with the literal place where we were located. Given the collapse of the steel industry in the 1980s, Hamilton struggles to find new ways of life in a post-steel economy. What this means is that our region is reevaluating its basic narratives—of why the city remains here, what kinds of livelihood are possible, how to facilitate healthy futures in a time of transition, how to relate to and restore polluted and desecrated land. With many old industrial buildings and warehouses empty, many people from the neighboring metropolis of Toronto, just seventy kilometers (roughly forty-four miles) from here, have seen opportunities to establish small businesses and art studios at cheaper rents. New community narratives on buttons and T-shirts declare "Art is the New Steel," "He said he liked it dirty, so we moved to Hamilton," or "You can do *anything* in Hamilton." Despite the humor and hyperbole, these slogans underline for us how significant community narratives can be—not only in reflecting community experiences but also in shaping possible futures, especially when a region is trying to negotiate significant change.

Four Sample CCENA Projects

This is the context in which CCENA took shape, and in the preceding pages, we have described the incremental process by which we derived a name for our center from long table consultations with a wide range of local and more-distant community experimenters and activists, and we have outlined the key principles we have been learning as we go. In this final section, we will briefly describe four of the eighteen projects with which we have partnered in the first two and a half years of CCENA's existence. In vetting project proposals with our Advisory Board, we relied upon four criteria: the project in question should (1) generate community-engaged narrative arts (i.e., stimulate new stories or new ways of collecting old stories); (2) provide a platform for the long-term sustaining or archiving of community-engaged narrative arts; (3) emphasize cognitive justice among different ways of knowing and intellectual emancipation (i.e., affirm and free up the intelligences that community people already have); and (4) take place in and be relevant to the Hamilton region. This sampling of four projects will convey a sense of the generic diversity of CCENA projects, reaching from oral poetry and visual creation narratives to photographic activism and place-based conceptual art. They also illustrate how we continue to shape and adapt our understanding of the power and potential of community-engaged narrative arts. Right from the start of CCENA, we heard repeatedly from people working to generate community narratives that it is very difficult to find time to do this kind of work in evenings and weekends after the regular workday. For people working in the arts, time is a research infrastructure, as crucial as time in the laboratory is to scientists and engineers; indeed, in a reversal of the saying "time is money," so obvious as to seem hardly worth saying, the primary item that research funding can provide for scholars in the humanities and arts is time—time to read, time to write, time to create. So, in consultation with our advisory committee, we decided that CCENA could offer fellowships that would cover creative workers' salaries while they took time off from work and devoted their full attention to projects that had been delayed repeatedly by their day jobs. Our first fellowship was with Rick Hill, a Tuscarora artist, curator, cultural historian, and Haudenosaunee knowledge holder who lives on Six Nations of the Grand River. Hill has had a long career in the arts and, in particular, in the restoration and regeneration of Haudenosaunee arts, having served as museum curator and director at many institutions, including the Institute of American Indian Arts, Santa Fe, and the National Museum of the American Indian in Washington, DC. Over the years of his career, he had collected interviews with Haudenosaunee artists, and he needed to set aside some time to complete the manuscript of a book he had been preparing on Six Nations visual artists' renderings of their traditional Creation Story. Hamilton is located in traditional Haudenosaunee territory, and we felt that as one of our first projects, it would be important to support the completion of this manuscript that engages with the origin stories of this region. When he visited our long table gathering, Hill reminded us that creation stories explain how we see the world, not in abstract philosophy but in grounded, ecologically specific terms—which is another way of saying that they are also about how the world sees us and our future. The Haudenosaunee Creation Story, like other Indigenous origin stories, highlights reciprocity between humans and the environment—when plants and animals cooperate in providing sustenance for Sky Woman after she falls into our present cosmos. Hill wanted to learn from the artists he interviewed how they understand and interpret this ancient story. Because of many factors, including residential schools,

Figure 3. One of the works reproduced in Rick Hill's book. Shelley Niro, Kanien'kehaka (Mohawk), *Skywoman*, 2001. Foam, fiberglass resin, oil paint, canvas, and metal. *Source*: Canadian Museum of Civilization, 2000.129.1.1-10, D2004-11229.

adoption into non-Indigenous families, mainstream education, and the saturation of mass media in everybody's homes, including Indigenous ones, many of the artists grew up without connections to traditional communities or knowledge, so in his interviews, Hill asks how the artists relearned this knowledge and how they wish to communicate it through dialogical forms that bring together Indigenous art traditions and Western ones. His purpose is to draw together and curate a Haudenosaunee art community, so that artists of different generations, regions, and levels of access to traditional knowledge can understand their work in dialogue with one another. He also wants the book to inform a wider public about the teachings carried within the Creation Story. The book therefore opens with a retelling of the Story and then presents a survey of Haudenosaunee philosophy in addition to the Haudenosaunee beadwork, pottery, and decorative needlework that derive from it. The book next turns to a discussion of the art works of his interviewees, alongside color reproductions of their works (see figure 3). In this way, the book fosters the idea of a "school" of Haudenosaunee art brought together with Haudenosaunee scholarship.

Over the course of his fellowship, Hill completed the manuscript, and we then edited it. The next stage of this project is to enter into dialogue with Haudenosaunee scholars who are studying the forty-some written versions of the Creation Story collected by anthropologists and Haudenosaunee people themselves since the eighteenth century. According to Hill, some of the most widely published of these written texts have influenced the ways in which Haudenosaunee elders themselves tell the story, so that, over time, it is possible to see the oral and written versions of the Creation Story weave back and forth, influencing one another. Part of the point of Hill's work is not to winnow the story down to an "authoritative" version but to remind people in the present of the dynamic multiplicity, adaptability, and richness of that tradition. The visual renderings of the Creation Story offer a powerful way to navigate between the oral tradition, enabled by material culture arts such as beadwork, wampum, pottery, sculpture, and basketry, and the wealth of written materials that can ensure a dynamic future for Haudenosaunee traditional knowledge.

The activist, community-based performances of Hamilton dub poet Klyde Broox have given rise to another CCENA-sponsored initiative that, like Rick Hill's Haudenosaunee Creation Story project, testifies to the power of time-release fellowships to support the objectives of already-ongoing community-knowledge production. In 1993, Klyde Broox brought with him to Hamilton the rich dub traditions in which he worked as a poet in Jamaica: "the blending," as he says in the introduction to his collection *My Best Friend Is White*, "of musical, literary, and oral storytelling devices with vernacular speech rhythms" that is "rooted in Rasta/reggae tradition" (7). Since the 1990s, Broox has been a crucial part of the vibrant dub scene in southern Ontario, which is home to the second-largest concentration of dub poets in the world (after Jamaica). He has dedicated himself to the potential of dub to energize community activism and foster the kinds of intellectual emancipation that lie at the heart of the mandates of groups like Execo, InWithForward, and PosAbilities (see figure 4). Broox has worked tirelessly with many communities, from seasonal migrant workers to patients at the Hamilton Psychiatric Hospital to youth groups (one such group was called STEP UP, which stands for Speech That Enlightens People Uplifts Places). Indeed, Broox's creative practice epitomizes CCENA's commitment to place-based research. He coined the term *see-hear* to describe the process of speaking a language connected to place/"here"; as he told Susan Gingell, "One grounding for my concept of see-hear aesthetics is this

Dancing with the Inductive   135

Figure 4. Klyde Broox. *Source*: Lorraine York.

summoning of attention to the realities of a particular place at a particular historical time in the hope the person or people summoned will see a situation from another's point of view; but, as the pun in my spelling of the phrase *see-hear aesthetics* suggests, another crucial dimension to such aesthetics is reliance on *sounded* words as well as *printed* ones" (34). Broox's pun is richly multilayered, for we might "hear" the phrases "see-hear," "see here!" or, indeed, "*sea here*," the latter brilliantly evoking the primacy of the sea in Caribbean political and cultural history; as Birgit Neumann and Jan Rupp observe, "[I]t is time and time again the sea, as site of the Middle Passage and as a marker of island experiences, of displacement and belonging, which gives shape to an inherently polyvalent poetics of location" (472).

The fellowship that Klyde Broox received from CCENA allowed him to devote time to a new dub form: the performance essay. As Broox explains, it is "an unorthodox blend of expressive and expository elements simultaneously illustrating and explicating (dub)poetry as 'word-sound-and-shape-systems-engineering,' a veritable oral-scribal technology of the voice" ("Dejavoodoo"). He produces text in performance, orally first and foremost, and then incorporates certain aspects of that text in later versions of the oral performance/written essay. In so doing, Broox simultaneously performs and teaches dub, productively smudging the boundaries between creativity and pedagogy. The projected outcome of this project is a collection of performance essays, *Dubrakadabra et Cetera: Technologies of the Voice!* As in his previous poetic practice, Broox will challenge hierarchies of language and what he calls "spliterature" (the splitting of oral and written literatures), championing the oral but seeing it in dialectical exchange with print (as he has previously phrased it, "[T]he scripting of orality and the oralizing of scribality"; 7), and exploring transcultural and transnational alliances, with dub holding out the possibility of exchange across cultures in a "Tellurian common ground." But the poetry is also intensely local in its globality; as Broox observes, he performs a poetry of "incident" as dub poetry traditionally does, finding much of its energy and impetus in responses to local community happenings and social-justice causes. The connections between *Dubrakadabra* and the notions of intellectual emancipation and epistemological justice that CCENA has come to embrace as foundational ideas are clear and compelling.

Alongside the fellowships for Rick Hill and Klyde Broox, CCENA has also partnered with various community organizations and individuals to provide small grants that enable them to carry out their narrative-making projects. Two of these were art and photography projects that highlight how narrative-making participates powerfully in creating the social glue that builds communities: the first was a retrospective project on over forty years of photographic works by Cees and Annerie van Gemerden, who are now in their seventies and not actively exhibiting their work anymore, and the second was a project entitled *Something Round*, in which the artist Margaret Flood collected round objects collected by hikers she met on the Bruce Trail. In the first project, CCENA partnered with Paul Lisson and Fiona Kinsella, editors of the local online magazine *Hamilton Arts and Letters*, to pay the rights for reproducing a selection of the van Gemerdens' photos in the magazine and to offer honoraria for eight authors to write essays that provided biographical background, set their work in relationship to the history of the photography of everyday life (in the *James Street North* series), examined the impact of their activist politics in the city through photo series that addressed pollution of the city's waterfront (*No Trespassing—*

More Power Anyone? series), the building of an expressway through the environmentally sensitive Red Hill Valley, a site declared sacred by Haudenosaunee people (*Red Hill* series), and the poverty of artists in the city under the austerity measures of the provincial governments of the 1990s (*The Dirty '90s* series). CCENA helped the magazine host a launch for the van Gemerden issue of *Hamilton Arts and Letters* at the Hamilton Public Library, an event that included an exhibition of their work and gathered a crowd of about two hundred and fifty people to witness the authors of the magazine essays discuss the van Gemerdens' impact, not only through their photography but also through their central involvement since the 1980s in Hamilton Artists Inc. and the Hamilton Photographer's Union and to celebrate their receipt of a Lifetime Achievement Award presented by the local MP (member of the Parliament of Canada), David Christopherson. At the same time, a more extensive exhibition of their photos was showing at *b contemporary*, an art gallery a few blocks from the public library. The event and the special issue of the magazine demonstrate very palpably how stories make communities and communities make stories. (Please see the issue at http://samizdatpress.typepad.com/hal_magazine_issue_nine2/hal-magazine-issue-nine2-cover-index.html.)

One of the stories repeated most fondly about the van Gemerdens tells of how they were irked when they settled in Hamilton in 1984 to see a fence posted with No Trespassing signs keeping residents from visiting the city's extensive harbor. They therefore photographed the fence itself, the many people who disregarded the signs and created trails down to the waterfront, and, most importantly, the toxic waste that private companies had dumped there (see figure 5).

Gathering seventy-five of these photos, the van Gemerdens created an exhibition called *No Trespassing—More Power Anyone?*, which revealed the industrial abuse that had led the Ministry of the Environment to designate the waterfront a toxic waste site. The exhibition was first shown at Hamilton Artists Inc. in 1989 and later as part of a Greenpeace show entitled *No Time to Waste* at the Hamilton Convention Centre, but the Art Gallery of Hamilton chose not to exhibit it. As Cees van Gemergen told David Forsee, "The problem . . . is that if you hide history, hide what has gone before, then people cannot learn from it" (n.p.). Resisting the city's desire to hide its toxic history, the van Gemerdens decided, during summer Aquafest in 1990, to mount their own exhibition where it could not be hidden: on the very fence their photos protested (see figure 6).

Figure 5. "Tree Versus Battery Cases" by Cees van Gemerden. *Source*: Cees van Gemerden.

The resulting widespread abhorrence at politicians' collusion in private industries' abuse of what should be public waterfront generated the political will for the city of Hamilton to purchase the property, carry out an environmental clean-up and remove the fence, and today Waterfront and Pier Four Parks welcome visitors to enjoy bike paths, native landscaping, benches, and play areas where once broken batteries had been illegally dumped. As Forsee concludes in his essay: "We need the work of Cees and Annerie, and the artists of James Street North then and the artists now to give us a way to remember, and to help us move forward wisely as a community during this time of great change" (n.p.).

Not all of the van Gemerdens' photographs are as publically situated as the exhibition of their activist photos on the waterfront fence. Much of their work documents the workings of everyday life, the labor of inner-city people, the struggles these people endure under austerity politics, the domestic

Figure 6. The general public chance upon the *No Trespassing* installation at Hamilton's Aquafest, 1990. *Source*: Annerie van Gemerden.

scenes where Hamiltonians create comfort and community. In her essay on their *James Street North* series, Mary O'Connor writes:

> As we see more and more of these photographs we build a sense of a community of place, and indeed one of the gifts of this series-making is the portrait of a street given back to those photographed.... Their work stands as an archive of cultural memory, one that is usually not told and not remembered. Their projects that chronicle time and place in the home, on the street or in the barred private lands of industry will be remembered as resisting and inspiring models of engaged art, art that includes and produces community. (n.p.)

This is precisely the kind of community-based art making that CCENA has been learning from even as we invest in it: the stories not usually told or remembered that, in fact, constitute important archives, not just of cultural memory but of alternatives for the future. For as our work with *Hamilton Arts and Letters* on the van Gemerden project demonstrates, there is a catalytic energy that grows when stories are recollected and retold: in the summer of 2018, less than two years after the launch of the magazine at which the van Gemerdens were honored and their stories retold, a significant retrospective of their work, featuring images from No Trespassing, went on exhibition at the Art Gallery of Hamilton.

Precious time freed up for creativity was a central feature of CCENA's support for a project by the Hamilton artist Margaret Flood. Flood, who came to Hamilton in 2012 after having earned her BFA from the Nova Scotia College of Art and Design and an MFA from the University of Guelph, is an interdisciplinary artist whose previous work has explored the relationship between everyday objects and autobiographical narrative. Her project called Some of My Parts, for instance, consisted of a set of measuring utensils that she fashioned in proportion to her bodily orifices. The series, which included a set of photographic representations of the measurement process, offered, in Flood's words, "an individualized measurement of the self as a collection of volumes" and explores "domesticity by turning an average kitchen utensil into a corporeal object" ("Hamilton Artists Inc. Newsletter"). Such an intensive concern with storytelling and the everyday marks a powerful point of intersection with CCENA's dedication to narratives of the locally embodied.

In recent years, Flood's practice has moved closer to that of conceptual art. As she has observed, her art has become "more idea-based and less about an object"; indeed, she has embraced the conceptual artist's move away from permanent art-object statements: "I love temporary things. I love the thought of nothing being permanent. I really reject striving for things that last forever" ("Living Arts Hamilton"). Flood's evolving practice dovetails with CCENA's commitment to story as malleable, multi-layered, and diversely communal. In 2016–17, CCENA supported a project by Flood that brought these commitments to the fore: Something Round. Flood has cited the walking trails that form part of the Bruce Trail system as "a big draw for me" when she decided to relocate to Hamilton ("Living Arts Hamilton"). In Something Round, she explores the ways in which the trails, which are part of an 890 kilometer (roughly 553-mile) -long walking-trail system from Niagara Falls to Tobermory, Ontario, have become fundamental, not only to her personal sense of locale and belonging but also to that of a whole community of individuals who frequent the trails. With the support offered by CCENA, Flood was able to spend long hours walking the local portion of the Bruce Trail and, when she met other trail users, she asked them if they would be willing to collect round objects that they found or saw on the trail and to offer their reflections about these found objects. In her words,

"Something Round" is an exhibition about walking, solitude and social interaction. Prompted by a curiosity about how people move through and relate to shared spaces, "Something Round" explores the perceptions and experiences of an unnamed – and possibly not self-identified–community formed by users of the Bruce Trail in Hamilton. Using photographs, narrative and a collection of circular detritus, Something Round considers the Bruce Trail as observed by a community of trail users. (Flood)

We were delighted to provide foundational support for this original project, which gained a broad local audience when it was exhibited, first at the Hamilton gallery The Assembly from 8–30 September 2017, and then at the Hamilton Public Library in July 2018. And we were even more delighted when Margaret Flood won the 2017 City of Hamilton Visual Arts Award in the Emerging Artist category in 2017.

Photographic materials from *Something Round* are still viewable at the Instagram account @somethinground, but in keeping with Flood's artistic practice of valuing the ephemeral over the monumental, we should note that she emphasized in the long table presentation she made on the project in February 2018 that she considers the narratives and the experiences of the trail users that emerged from her conversations with them on the trail as the heart of the project. The photographs, which we found stunningly beautiful in their own right (see figure 7), were, to Flood, secondary traces, though visually interesting ones, of the community-engaged narratives that coalesced to form *Something Round*.

Conclusion

We could never have conceived of projects like these if we considered literary scholarship something we did exclusively in solitude. Think of what would have been missed if we had tried to lay out the objectives and procedures of CCENA before actually engaging with these various creative community-based artists and writers! We needed to meet people like Margaret Flood, Paul Lisson and Fiona Kinsella, Klyde Broox, and Rick Hill in order even to conceive of a framework that would enable this kind of community-based narrative making. Our partners' longer experience of working in their communities, in addition to the extensive networks of people and institutions (from individuals to community organizations to public institutions and politicians) gave them not just the vision but also the

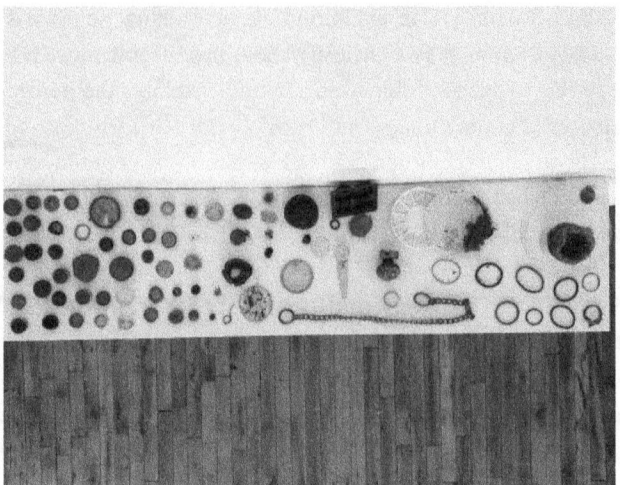

Figure 7. Margaret Flood, *Something Round*. Source: Wendy Coleman.

capacity to carry out this range of diverse but interrelated arts-based community-making projects. Despite our partners' remarkable resourcefulness, however, we also have learned that they needed CCENA to help them contact essay writers, to afford fees and honoraria, and to publicize their events beyond their own networks. Working with them, we learned what we suspected but only saw through active collaboration: that community-based narrative artists are already at work. They are not looking to universities to send them faculty or graduate students to either invent or research a project for them. Rather, they look to those of us who work at universities to see and affirm the value of the stories and archives they are already generating and to do this in practical ways: to help them afford things that to university researchers are no huge challenge but to them are usually out of reach; the ability to pay artists, writers, and editors; to afford basic equipment such as computers or cameras; to pay honoraria; to book meeting spaces whose fees are usually prohibitive but are often free to university researchers; to qualify for grants and public-arts funding; and to afford creators necessary time to work on the projects themselves. What we have learned in the first few years CCENA has existed has been not so much how to generate these projects but rather how to come alongside, to participate in what intellectually emancipating communities are already doing, and—like any good dancer—to follow their lead.

Note

1. Thank you to Dr. Simon Orpana for encouraging us to clarify the implications of our use of this term.

Works Cited

Blair, Jennifer, Daniel Coleman, Kate Higginson, and Lorraine York, editors. *Re-Calling Early Canada: Reading the Political in Literary and Cultural Production*. U of Alberta P, 2005.

Broox, Klyde. *My Best Friend Is White*. McGilligan Books, 2005.

Coleman, Daniel, and Smaro Kamboureli "Introduction to Canadian Research Capitalism: A Genealogy of Critical Moments." *Retooling the Humanities: The Culture of Research in Canadian Universities*, edited by Coleman and Kamboureli, U of Alberta P, 2011, pp. 1–39.

Deane, Patrick. "Forward with Integrity." McMaster University, 21 Sep. 2011.

Estrada, Andrea. "Musical Improvisation as a Tool for Social Change." *The Current: Society and Culture (UC Santa Barbara)*, 28 Oct. 2013, http://www.news.ucsb.edu/2013/013655/musical-improvisation-tool-social-change.

Flood, Margaret. "Something Round." *Akimbo*, http://www.akimbo.ca/akimbos/?id=109888. Accessed 30 Jul. 2018.

Forsee, David. "Cees and Annerie van Gemerden: Life as a Work of Art." *Hamilton Arts & Letters*, vol. 9, no. 2, 2016–2017, http://samizdatpress.typepad.com/hal_magazine_issue_nine2/hal-magazine-issue-nine2-cover-index.html.

Gingell, Susan. "Coming Home through Sound: See-Hear Aesthetics in the Poetry of Louise Bennett and Canadian Dub Poets." *Journal of West Indian Literature*, vol. 17, no. 2, 2009, pp. 32–48.

Gruenewald, David A. "The Best of Both Worlds: A Critical Pedagogy of Place." *Educational Researcher*, vol. 32, no. 4, May 2003, pp. 3–12.

"Hamilton Artists Inc. Newsletter." *Hamilton Artists Inc.*, 2015, http://www.theinc.ca/wp-content/uploads/2015/05/newsletter-summer2015.pdf.

Jackson, Elizabeth. *Community-University Engagement in Canada: Voices from the Field*. McMaster Institute for Excellence in Teaching and Learning, 2014.

Justice, Daniel Heath. *Why Indigenous Literatures Matter*. Wilfrid Laurier Press, 2018.

King, Martin Luther, Jr. "Nonviolence: The Only Road to Freedom." 1966. *A Testament of Hope: The Essential Writings of Martin Luther King, Jr.*, edited by James Melvin Washington, Harper and Row, 1986, pp. 54–61.

Lipsitz, George. "Arts-Based Community Making in Black and Chicano Communities." International Institute for Critical Studies in Improvisation (University of Guelph), http://improvisationinstitute.ca/research-project/arts-based-community-making-in-black-and-chicano-communities/. Accessed 30 Jul. 2018.

"Living Arts Hamilton Podcast: Margaret Flood." *Hamilton Arts Council*, 20 Sep. 2015, https://hamiltonartscouncil.ca/livingarts/podcast/margaret-flood.

Monture, Rick. *We Share Our Matters: Two Centuries of Writing and Resistance at Six Nations of the Grand River*. U of Manitoba P, 2014.
Neumann, Birgit, and Jan Rupp. "Sea Passages: Cultural Flows in Caribbean Poetry." *Atlantic Studies*, vol. 13, no. 4, 2016, pp. 472–90.
O'Connor, Mary. "Chronicles of Space and Time: The Photographic Projects of Cees and Annerie van Gemerden." *Hamilton Arts & Letters*, vol. 9, no. 2, 2016–2017, http://samizdatpress.typepad.com/hal_magazine_issue_nine2/hal-magazine-issue-nine2-cover-index.html.
Santos, Boaventura de Sousa, João Arriscado Nunes, and Maria Paula Meneses. "Introduction: Opening Up the Canon of Knowledge and Recognition of Difference." *Another Knowledge Is Possible: Beyond Northern Epistemologies*, edited by de Sousa Santos, Verso, 2007, pp. xix–lxii.
Shorris, Earl. "In the Hands of the Restless Poor." *Harper's Magazine*, Sep. 1997, pp. 50–59.
Tanti, Melissa, Jeremy Haynes, Daniel Coleman, and Lorraine York, editors. *Beyond Understanding Canada: Transnational Perspectives on Canadian Literature*. U of Alberta P, 2017.

Conclusion

Literary Study Writ Large

Rosemary Erickson Johnsen

***Public Scholarship in Literary Studies* is grounded in, and a demonstration of, the conviction that literary scholars possess a combination of knowledge base and specialist skills with enormous potential for public scholarship.** Similar to the ways in which public scholars in the field of history rely on, and further develop, their training in historiography and their rich historical knowledge in a specialist area, so too do scholars in literature have both a *data set* and a *skill set* that position them to make strong contributions to public life. As the contributions to this volume demonstrate, literary criticism has the potential not only to explain but to actively change our terms of engagement with current realities. Their ongoing, career-long accumulation of specialist knowledge positions literary scholars to speak not just to other scholars and students, but directly to the public. We should never lose sight of the facts that "disciplinary grounding . . . is a key asset" (Parker 469) and that literary scholars enjoy an enormous resource: literature itself.

Literary scholars should be alert and receptive to opportunities created by current events to share our expertise with public audiences. One such opportunity manifested itself for me in the wake of the 2016 election, when the term *gaslighting* achieved an unfortunate new currency. I wrote an essay for *The Los Angeles Review of Books* (*LARB*) in 2017 that examined Patrick Hamilton's 1938 stage play *Gaslight: A Victorian Thriller* as the original source of the term. In Hamilton's hands, an observation about the functioning of Victorian home gaslight systems is transformed into a compelling dramatic device and eventually became shorthand for the process of driving a person to question their own sanity through deliberate psychological manipulation. In the *LARB* article, my knowledge base as a literary scholar rectifies misapprehensions and uses the tools of literary criticism to illuminate additional dimensions of the term and its inception. I still have to explain who Hamilton is—that has been true since he became the subject of my doctoral dissertation in 1997—but my knowledge of the late 1930s context and his dramatic vision in *Gaslight* now finds newly receptive audiences.

Twenty-first-century historians have enjoyed some success in demonstrating the renewed relevance of history to understanding the present epoch in politics and cultural change, speaking out in op-eds and as #twitterstorians. Since the middle of the last decade, several canonical literary texts have been invoked as sharing parallels with contemporary society such George Orwell's *Nineteen Eighty-Four*, Margaret Atwood's *The Handmaid's Tale*, and William Golding's *The Lord of the Flies*. Popular use of adjectives such as *Orwellian* and *dystopian* signals an opportunity for experts in Orwell or the dystopia to enrich public discourse; these scholars have information we can use right now. Christopher Douglas's chapter in this collection describes and dissects this process, one in which knowledge that may have appeared arcane and of interest only to readers of university press studies becomes timely for a much broader audience. The specialist knowledge and disciplinary training that informs his Cornell University Press book, *If God Meant to Interfere: American Literature and the Rise of the Christian Right*, also informs the pieces he has written for what we might call a readership of educated citizens. Scholars in literary fields know how much there is to learn from literature; the inclusion of public scholarship in our professional profiles allows us to share such learning beyond our disciplinary communities and classrooms.

Scholars can add depth to public engagement with known texts of interest, but they can also use their training to broaden the set of relevant source material. Critical theory is much maligned outside of the academy, but it offers ways of seeing that are valuable. If no one is calling out for examples of its use, that does not mean a literary scholar cannot deploy it alongside knowledge of primary-source material, literary history (including knowledge of genre developments and changing critical reception), and expert skills in dissecting complex texts. General-audience awareness of what literary scholars know and do is the tip of the iceberg, and public scholarship can reveal just how much else is beneath the surface: familiarity with canonical and lesser-known texts and authors, knowledge of cultural and historical context, and the ability to make connections across times, places, and texts. People often invoke *Nineteen Eighty-Four*, yes, but how much more could Orwell's novel be illuminated by accessible literary analysis and context? And what of lesser-known material that could inform public discourse?

When it comes to public scholarship in literary studies, the trajectory of the work and the scholar are intertwined. The arc of Carmaletta M. Williams's career in Kansas, brought to life in her chapter for this volume, reveals how her academic career, her public engagement, and her own scholarship are inextricably linked. In "Takin' It to the Streets: Public Scholarship in the Heartland," Williams forthrightly shows the challenges, risks, and rewards of her engagement with the public and, in so doing, offers inspiration to others to take courage and go forth. As she and the other contributors indicate, the practitioner is part of the story of public engagement, and the history of my own engagement with public scholarship supports the platform from which I speak. That history also sheds light on the multiplicities of literary study as public scholarship. If we look, we can often discern in the motivations and activities of individuals' professional engagements broader patterns or pivotal moments in the arena of public scholarship. I would like to offer some key moments from my own public-scholarship trajectory in order to demonstrate my long-standing commitment to the subject of this volume but, more importantly, because I believe doing so illuminates the complicated webs of engagement typical for those pursuing public scholarship.

I first encountered the term *public scholarship* when I served on the Modern Language Association's Committee on the Status of Women in the Profession (CSWP) from 2008 to 2011. Having been engaged in public scholarship for some years without benefit of the nomenclature, the term was not simply a useful marker but a way to begin drilling down into its definition: Where does one draw the lines in defining the boundaries of public scholarship? At that time, efforts were being made to get "public scholarship" recognized as a category of activity distinct from service, freelancing, or personal-interest activity. The MLA's CSWP identified it as an issue with particular significance for women scholars, and the committee sponsored panels on the topic at the annual convention during the period of my committee service. My initial acquaintance with the term was significant for me personally in terms of taking my own "community engagement" seriously, but it is also a broader reflection of movements then afoot.

In 2012, I took another step forward in public engagement by establishing my own Web site. Web presence was a standard expectation for academics by then, but my own university exerted such tight control over the content that I realized I needed to create and manage my own. I consulted a colleague in my university's College of Business, selected and registered a domain name, and signed a contract for web hosting with a commercial provider. Designing the site, creating and updating the content, learning how to solve problems, and add features: all of these things took me into new territory. The following year, when I signed on to Twitter (at the behest of the director of the sculpture park on the grounds of my university's campus), I learned how to make the Web site and my Twitter presence work together. Five years after that, when I was directing an NEH project, I had those two outlets in place to make multidirectional engagement easier and more visible. By the time I was presenting at the Society for the Advancement of Scandinavian Study on how to use Twitter for public-humanities engagement in 2019, I had come a long way. If now I see that my Web site is in need of a redesign, that, too, is part of the process! Like my introduction to the terminology of public scholarship, my experiences in establishing a cyber presence were natural reflections of broader developments, as are the connections between those activities and my commitment to public scholarship.

My 2015 article "Public Scholarship: Making the Case" in *Modern Language Studies* was a case study of my experience serving as scholar for several productions at a Chicago-area theater. The moment captured in that article is one of transition: the MLA had begun encouraging members to use public engagement as a way to advocate for the value of MLA mission-centric research, teaching, and engagement, and the National Endowment for the Humanities had recently announced the creation of an initiative called the Common Good: The Humanities in the Public Square. In 2015, there was a pressing need to "make the case" for public-facing literary criticism to the public, to campus evaluators, and to colleagues within the discipline. There were a limited number of scholarly articles published at that time, and venues such as *The Chronicle of Higher Education*, professional associations, and community and government agencies offered material of value to those trying to better understand and define their engagements with public scholarship. *Imagining America* published "Scholarship in Public: Knowledge Creation and Tenure Policy in the Engaged University: A Resource on Promotion and Tenure in the Arts, Humanities, and Design"

(Ellison and Eatman) as long ago as 2008, and the American Historical Association adopted "Tenure, Promotion, and the Publicly Engaged Academic Historian" in 2010, with substantial revisions in 2017. Professional associations in the humanities and social sciences continue to raise their level of commitment to research into, and support for, public scholarship, which in turn bolsters attempts being made at individual institutions to bring standards for public engagement into tenure processes. The upswing in public engagement has been fueled in part by a changing political landscape, which has only increased the urgency to show how our disciplinary work can have meaning for many publics. The multitudinous ways people with advanced training and professional qualifications in literary study make their living in a time of waning support for higher education extends our understanding of what public scholarship might look like and how it can be built into institutional structures, including, but going beyond, those afforded to college and university faculty.

There are signs that this shift in valuation is underway. Increasing recognition of the need for it can be seen in a variety of grant programs—for example, including NEH programs directed at public scholarship. In founding its Public Scholars program, the NEH "entered a long-term commitment to encourage scholarship in the humanities for general audiences" (NEH). Our contributors in this volume include a 2018 NEH public scholar, Cynthia L. Haven, whose chapter demonstrates the impact of her work, grounded in the practices of literary criticism, on international audiences. Beyond its directly designated grants for public scholarship, the NEH has several other initiatives that underwrite and amplify what can be considered public scholarship. In 2017, I was awarded the first of two NEH grants I received under the auspices of the Dialogues on the Experience of War (DEW) program, part of Standing Together: The Humanities and the Experience of War initiative launched in the spring of 2014 (the same year the Common Good was announced). The DEW program is part of the Education Division of the NEH, and the two projects I designed and delivered involved training student-veterans to serve as embedded discussion facilitators in credit-bearing university courses and then at a series of public events. The practice of literary criticism on a diverse set of war-related literature was enacted by the faculty codirectors and, more importantly, by the team of student-veterans. Under the auspices of the grants, the student-veterans were trained as discussion facilitators for the class and went on to engage audiences across campus and the surrounding community through the shared practice of literary criticism. Over the course of two projects (2017–19), the student-veteran team, course students, the codirectors, and others filmed a televised town hall event discussing humanities texts before a live audience; hosted a Veterans Day program on campus that included an open poetry discussion, veteran art exhibition, WWI panel discussion, and the premiere of a documentary film made by one of our 2017 student-veterans; and brought interactive humanities discussions to local sites, including a VFW post, public library, and community college. Instruction and practice in the tools of literary criticism, confidence in its value, and an ever-increasing knowledge base of primary sources helped establish these student-veterans as public scholars in their own right.

The public events and activities of the grant projects illustrate the potential of literary criticism to serve as meaningful, even transformative, public scholarship, and they represent the "multi-directional exchange of ideas" (Johnsen 9) characteristic of successful public scholarship grounded in literary study. Furthermore, the connections made through these projects, in tandem with my move to an administrative role at the university, illustrate how public scholarship often develops in a nonlinear way quite distinct from the traditional progression of literary scholarship in the academy. The literary criticism engaged in with diverse publics through the grant projects has benefited participants; it has also led to new kinds of professional engagement for me that are practice based and advocacy oriented, including presentations at conferences and interest groups for administrators, veterans affairs professionals, and veterans organizations. The practice of literary criticism was brought, through the grants, to individual members of the community and then, in turn, found openings for new avenues of institutionalization, such as the invitation we received to help a nearby regional comprehensive university learn how to incorporate literary study in its Green Zone training. These interconnections and opportunities all revolve around the public practice of literary analysis.

The time is right for *Public Scholarship in Literary Studies.* In the twenty-first-century landscape of growing institutional and civic imperatives for literary scholars to engage in public-facing dissemination of their work, our understanding of public scholarship in the humanities has undergone significant shifts. Increasingly, the professional organizations of many humanities and social-science disciplines are calling for their members to engage in public scholarship and are beginning to provide tools for academic evaluators to credit such work. As the practice of public scholarship has grown, its forms have multiplied. The contributors to this volume, writing out of their own experiences in the field, showcase best practices in a range of public-scholarship modes. Their contributions to praxis offer innovative models for those seeking to engage in public scholarship as newcomers or as longtime participants, and they provide rich material for use by those who seek to understand and/or evaluate public scholarship in the humanities. The editors are particularly pleased that this volume is being published on the digital-first open-access platform of Amherst College Press, and the collection is offered as an invitation for further conversation. It is also a call to action.

The power of literature to enrich and inform understanding is well known to literary scholars. Increasingly, however, that foundational truth is disregarded or actively attacked. Literature, like much of the humanities, is often spoken of as a luxury or, even worse, as useless. Bringing literary study into the realm of public scholarship can help counter those misperceptions, working both individually and collectively to restore some confidence in what we do as scholars of literature. Public scholarship becomes the means to share what literary scholarship offers, but also to chip away at the presence of anti-intellectualism in contemporary society. Our ability to serve as intermediary between text and audience—the kinds of work we routinely do in our classrooms and at campus events—positions us to contribute beyond campus and our scholarly communities and to learn from the perspectives and insights available from those who do not inhabit our campuses. Public scholarship often takes forms recognizably similar to teaching and learning, but it can also serve as advocacy. We need that now more than ever.

A few decades ago, Cora Kaplan conceptualized *political* for humanities scholars as a deliberate position in which "what is being taught . . . is being taught in relation to a dynamic of what you might *do* or *produce* or *be* in some future conjuncture, rather than just as an object of study" (21, original emphasis). The immediate context for Kaplan's definition was feminist scholarship in the academy, but I believe it's a vision that can invite literary scholars to embrace and create opportunities to be more adventurous in considering public forms for their research and teaching practice. What might public scholarship look like *now*, against a backdrop of a global pandemic, social-justice activism, and an evident need for critical engagement with texts of all kinds? The contributors to *Public Scholarship in Literary Studies* share their own trajectories that continue to adapt and develop;

their chapters offer personal experience, knowledge, and inspiration. If this volume's readers are inspired to embrace a forward-looking, active vision of engagement for public scholarship, we can change the world.

Works Cited

Ellison, Julie, and Timothy K. Eatman. "Scholarship in Public: Knowledge Creation and Tenure Policy in the Engaged University: A Resource on Promotion and Tenure in the Arts, Humanities, and Design." *Imagining America*, 2008, https://imaginingamerica.org/what-we-do/past-initiatives/.

Johnsen, Rosemary Erickson. "On the Origins of Gaslighting." *Los Angeles Review of Books*, 9 Mar. 2017, https://lareviewofbooks.org/article/on-the-origins-of-gaslighting/.

———. "Public Scholarship: Making the Case." *Modern Language Studies*, vol. 45, no. 1, 2015, pp. 8–19.

Kaplan, Cora. "Feminist Criticism Twenty Years On." *From My Guy to Sci-Fi: Genre and Women's Writing in the Postmodern World*, edited by Helen Carr, Pandora, 1989, pp. 15–23.

"NEH Creates New 'Public Scholar' Grant Program Supporting Popular Scholarly Books in the Humanities." National Endowment for the Humanities, press release, 1 Dec. 2014, https://www.neh.gov/news/press-release/2014-12-01.

Parker, Patricia., et al. "Decolonizing the Academy: Lessons from the Graduate Certificate in Participatory Research at the University of North Carolina at Chapel Hill." *Qualitative Inquiry*, 2017, tps://doi.org/10.1177/1077800417729846.

"Tenure, Promotion, and the Publicly Engaged Academic Historian." The American Historical Association, 2017, https://www.historians.org/jobs-and-professional-development/statements-standards-and-guidelines-of-the-discipline/tenure-promotion-and-the-publicly-engaged-academic-historian.

Appendix

Program Overviews

Centre for Community Engaged Narrative Arts (CCENA)

Those of us who participate in the Centre for Community Engaged Narrative Arts (CCENA) believe that addressing the inequities in our world depends upon widespread recognition of the inherent value of diverse communities' everyday experiential knowledge: their stories. CCENA aims to learn from the stories and narrative traditions through which communities imagine themselves and their relationships with each other. With this aim in mind, CCENA seeks to support and sustain art-based community listening, remembering, and story making. We link community members with other communities and with various media and sources of expertise in order to support them in telling their stories. CCENA works with:

- community groups, either existing or envisioned
- artists
- individual community members
- arts organizations
- public intellectuals

We take our lead from community initiatives, priorities, and needs, and seek to collaborate with those communities—in Hamilton, Ontario, and beyond—to work in the service of shared memory, sustainability, and creativity. In that spirit, we seek to bring together university resources (whether financial, cultural, infrastructural, or research) with community capacities, so that we can learn and retell the stories of living well together. Learn more at https://ccena.ca/.

Clemente Course in the Humanities

The Clemente Course in the Humanities inspires and equips motivated, low-income adults to take charge of their lives. Our yearlong program activates students' intelligence, fosters the skills to make informed decisions, and kindles the self-confidence to act upon them. Clemente uses the transformative experience of the humanities to spark a productive change in its students.

Clemente offers free, accredited humanities courses to underserved adults. The nine-month course meets weekly for four hours. The experience is rigorous, but the class is accessible to motivated and engaged individuals. Every student receives all of the course materials for free. Transportation and child care are also provided, removing crucial barriers to attendance. Since 1996, over ten thousand students have benefited from the Clemente Course in the Humanities.

Professors from leading colleges and universities teach every course, using the Socratic method. Class discussions, readings, and written assignments build skills in critical thinking, written and oral communications, time management, teamwork, and self-advocacy. College credits earned from a Clemente Course provide a springboard to higher education.

Learn more at https://clementecourse.org/.

Texts and Teachers

Texts and Teachers is a curriculum-development program and university/high school collaboration, based at the University of Washington in Seattle. It has been operating since 2000. The project offers dual-credit linked classes to more than four hundred high school students in ten area high schools each year. High school teachers are involved in designing courses to be taught, making them partners in a shared educational project. Participating teachers work with a University of Washington faculty member to design a new course in a summer workshop that is then taught on a regular basis at both the university and in high schools, with visits back and forth by University of Washington faculty and participating high school students. Learn more at https://simpsoncenter.org/.

Contributors

Editors

Rachel Arteaga is assistant director of the Simpson Center for the Humanities at the University of Washington, where she also serves as associate program director for Reimagining the Humanities PhD and Reaching New Publics, a public-scholarship initiative supported by the Andrew W. Mellon Foundation. Arteaga completed a PhD in English in 2016, specializing in American literature, and holds a certificate in public scholarship, both from the University of Washington. Her publications on higher education have appeared in the Modern Language Association journal *Profession* and *Inside Higher Ed*, and materials she has developed related to humanities curriculum and advocacy are accessible on *Humanities Commons*. Arteaga speaks and writes regularly on doctoral education, public scholarship, and the value of the humanities. She is a member of the advisory board of the Humanities, Arts, Science, and Technology Alliance and Collaboratory (HASTAC) and has served on planning and review committees for the National Endowment for the Humanities, the National Humanities Alliance, and Humanities Washington. She has supported and participated in a wide range of cross-institutional partnerships, working with teachers and instructors in the K–12 system, community colleges, and four-year colleges and universities to strengthen educational infrastructure and access to opportunity for students in the Pacific Northwest. The current volume was, in its earliest form, a special session she organized for the 2018 Modern Language Association convention in New York City. Further information is available at www.rachelarteaga.com.

Rosemary Erickson Johnsen is associate provost and associate vice president of academic affairs at Governors State University, in the Chicago metro area. She is the university's chief administrator of faculty affairs and served as the interim administrator for the university library (2020-21). She is a two-time recipient of grants from the National Endowment for the Humanities under the auspices of the Dialogues on the Experience of War program (2017; 2018). Also a professor of English, Johnsen has published a book, *Contemporary Feminist Historical Crime Fiction* (Palgrave Macmillan), and many articles on crime fiction, Irish literature, and public humanities. Other editorial work includes guest editing a theme issue on historical crime fiction for *Clues: A Journal of Detection*. Johnsen's public scholarship activities include appearing as guest scholar for four productions at Chicago's Tony Award-winning Lookingglass Theatre, and she has published essays in *The Los Angeles Review of Books*, *Mystery Tribune*, and other outlets. She has served on the editorial advisory board of the *Journal of Popular Culture* since 2008. A member of the Executive Council of the Society for the Advancement of Scandinavian Study, she is also a former cochair of the MLA's Committee on the Status of Women in the Profession. She is on Twitter @johnsenrm and maintains a website at http://rosemaryj.com.

Contributors

Christine Chaney is professor of English and director of the honors program at Seattle Pacific University, as well as affiliate assistant professor of English at the University of Washington (as part of the UW in the high school Texts and Teachers program). Her publications include contributions to *Victorian Hybridities: Cultural Anxiety and Formal Invention* (2010) and *Romantic Autobiography in England* (2009), along with several journal articles on narrative theory, Romantic and Victorian autobiography, and higher-education pedagogy. She is also one of the founding editors of *Pedagogy: Critical Approaches to Teaching Literature, Language, Composition, and Culture* (Duke University Press). She is currently at work on a book considering narrative ethics and Victorian socialism after a decade of faculty leadership in two general education-curricular-reform projects.

Jim Cocola is associate professor in the Department of Humanities and Arts at Worcester Polytechnic Institute (WPI) in Worcester, Massachusetts, where he also serves as academic director and poetry instructor in the local division of the Clemente Course in the Humanities, a program recognized internationally for bringing college-level humanities courses to people living in economic distress. Since the first Clemente Course was offered over thirty years ago, more than ten thousand adults have taken part in its seminars. In Worcester, with the sponsorship of the Massachusetts Foundation for the Humanities and under the direction of Professor Cocola, the program transforms literary criticism into public scholarship, bringing faculty expertise in literature into conversation with the life experiences of its students. At WPI, Cocola was recognized in 2015 with the Romeo L. Moruzzi Young Faculty Award for Innovation in Undergraduate Education. His first book, *Places in the Making: A Cultural Geography of American Poetry* (University of Iowa Press, 2016), won a Helen Tartar First Book Subvention Award from the American Comparative Literature Association.

Daniel Coleman is professor of English at McMaster University in Hamilton, Ontario, Canada. His teaching and research focus on Canadian literary cultures. He has published *Masculine Migrations* (1998), *The Scent of Eucalyptus* (2003), *White Civility* (2006; winner of the Raymond Klibansky prize), *In Bed with the Word* (2009), and *Yardwork: A Biography of an Urban Place* (2017, shortlisted for the RBC Taylor Prize). He has coedited nine volumes of literary and cultural criticism, the most recent of which are *Retooling the Humanities* (2011), *Countering Displacements* (2012), and, with Lorraine York, *Beyond Understanding Canada* (2017). He has long been fascinated by the poetic power of narrative arts to generate a sense of place and community, critical-social engagement and mindfulness, and especially wonder.

Christopher Douglas is professor of English at the University of Victoria, Canada, and is the author of *If God Meant to Interfere: American Literature and the Rise of the Christian Right*. His public scholarship on the intersections of literature, religion, and US politics has appeared in *Religion Dispatches*, *Marginalia*, and *The Conversation*. His Social Sciences and Humanities Research Council-funded research project is titled "Fundamentalist Fictions: God, Suffering and American Literature." His recent publications include "This Is The Shack That Job Built: Theodicy and Polytheism in William Paul Young's Evangelical Bestseller" in the *Journal of the American Academy of Religion* and guest-editing a special issue of *Christianity & Literature* on "Literature of / about the Christian Right." He can be found on *Twitter* at @crddouglas.

Contributors

Gary Handwerk is professor of English and comparative literature at the University of Washington, where he has just become director of UW's undergraduate program on the environment. His scholarship focuses on modern European narrative and narrative theory, narrative ethics, and ecocriticism. His publications include critical editions of William Godwin's *Caleb Williams* and *Fleetwood* (Broadview Press) and essays on several of Godwin's novels and on Rousseau's *Emile*. He is the translator and editor of Nietzsche's *Human, All Too Human* (Stanford University Press; volumes 1 [1995], 2 [2012], and 3 [2020]. For the last fifteen years, he has taught a course in environmental humanities, Living in Place, linked to several Seattle-area high schools.

Cynthia L. Haven is the author of *Evolution of Desire: A Life of René Girard*, the first biography of the French theorist. She was named a National Endowment for the Humanities public scholar in 2018. She writes regularly for *The Times Literary Supplement* and has also contributed to *The New York Times Book Review*, *The Nation*, *The Wall Street Journal*, *The Virginia Quarterly Review*, *The Washington Post*, *The Los Angeles Times*, *The San Francisco Chronicle*, and *World Literature Today*. Her work has also appeared in *Le Monde, La Repubblica, Die Welt, Zvezda, Colta, Zeszyty Literackie, The Kenyon Review, Quarterly Conversation, The Georgia Review*, and *Civilization*. She has been a Milena Jesenská journalism fellow with the Institut für die Wissenschaften vom Menschen in Vienna, as well as a visiting writer and scholar at Stanford's Division of Literatures, Cultures, and Languages and a Voegelin Fellow at Stanford's Hoover Institution. She has published several volumes on Nobel poets Czesław Miłosz, Joseph Brodsky, and others. She blogs at *The Book Haven* at http://bookhaven.stanford.edu/.

Anu Taranath brings both passion and expertise to her work as a speaker, facilitator, and educator. A professor at the University of Washington for the past eighteen years, she teaches about global literatures, race, gender, identity, and equity. A four-time member of the Humanities Washington Speakers Bureau, Taranath has also received *Seattle Weekly*'s "Best of Seattle" recognition, the UW's Distinguished Teaching Award, and multiple US Fulbright fellowships to work abroad. As a consultant and facilitator, Taranath engages colleges, universities, community organizations, businesses, and government agencies to deepen people's comfort with uncomfortable topics and work toward equity and social justice. Her book, *Beyond Guilt Trips: Mindful Travel in an Unequal World*, was published in 2019.

Carmaletta M. Williams is executive director of the Black Archives of Mid-America in Kansas City, Missouri. She taught courses in English and African American studies at Johnson County Community College in Kansas for over twenty-eight years, and she was the inaugural director of JCCC's Office of Diversity, Equity, and Inclusion. After retirement from JCCC, she spent a year in China teaching at Central China Normal University. Williams's research focuses on racial-identity formation, and her wide-ranging publications include family history, writers of the Harlem Renaissance, the letters of Langston Hughes, and literature for children. She won an Emmy for her portrayal of Harlem Renaissance–novelist, anthropologist, and folklorist Zora Neale Hurston on R. Crosby Kemper III's *Meet the Past* program on Kansas City Public TV in 2015.

Lorraine York is distinguished university professor in the Department of English and Cultural Studies at McMaster University. She is the author of *Literary Celebrity in Canada* (University of Toronto Press 2007), *Margaret Atwood and the Labour of Literary Celebrity* (University of Toronto 2013), and *Celebrity Cultures in Canada*, coedited with Katja Lee (Wilfrid Laurier University Press 2016). A recent book, *Reluctant Celebrity*, which examines public displays of celebrity reluctance as forms of privilege intertwined with race, gender, and sexuality, was published by Palgrave Macmillan in 2018. Throughout her career, she has been absorbed by the public performance of literary culture.

www.ingramcontent.com/pod-product-compliance
Lightning Source LLC
Chambersburg PA
CBHW060353110426
42743CB00036B/2905